STARTING YOUR
CAREER AS A
PROFESSIONAL
BLOGGER

JACQUELINE BODNAR

ALLWORTH PRESS
NEW YORK

Allworth Press books may be purchased in bulk at special discounts for sales promotion, corporate gifts, fund-raising, or educational purposes. Special editions can also be created to specifications. For details, contact the Special Sales Department, Allworth Press, 307 West 36th Street, 11th Floor, New York, NY 10018 or info@skyhorsepublishing.com.

17 16 15 14 13   5 4 3 2 1

Published by Allworth Press, an imprint of Skyhorse Publishing, Inc.
307 West 36th Street, 11th Floor, New York, NY 10018.

Allworth Press® is a registered trademark of Skyhorse Publishing, Inc.®, a Delaware corporation.

www.allworth.com

Cover design by Irvin Rodriguez

Library of Congress Cataloging-in-Publication Data is available on file.
ISBN: 978-1-62153-245-3

Printed in the United States of America

STARTING YOUR

CAREER AS A

PROFESSIONAL
BLOGGER

This book is dedicated to my mom, Linda, for raising me to believe I can do anything I put my mind to.

Contents

CONTENTS

CONTENTS

Preface

The integration of the Internet into our daily lives has brought a plethora of new career fields. People are working in fields that just a decade or two ago didn't exist. Today people can work from the comfort of their own homes in positions that run the gamut from software engineers to eBay store owners. There are many possibilities!

One of the new opportunities today is becoming a professional blogger. The Internet has created the entire field of blogging, where people can share information about something they are passionate about, become reporters that focus on a particular genre, and more. Individuals and businesses alike have found that blogs can provide a lot of value and benefits.

Becoming a professional blogger is not only obtainable and within reach, but it's also an emerging field that is only going to continue to grow. You are entering the field at a great time. It has been around long enough that we know what it takes to be successful, but it's new enough that you can still help pave the way for the future of blogging.

Professional blogging is an easy and low-cost profession to enter, yet it can pay off well. It doesn't require any particular types of degrees or training and you don't need a "license to blog." You can simply choose your focus, register a URL, and get started. The sky is the limit when it comes to how much you can earn as a professional blogger. Some bloggers make hundreds per month, but others make thousands per week. The more you learn about the salary-generating opportunities for bloggers, the more you can put them into action creating a name for yourself and earning a living from your efforts. There are bloggers who are making more money working for themselves than they ever did in nine-to-five jobs working for someone else. With blogging you get to be your own boss, work from home, set your own rates, and take on as much, or as little, work as you would like to, thus having more control over your yearly salary.

In the pages of this book you will find the information you need to go from no blogging experience to becoming a professional blogger and earning a living as you do it. You will learn how to get started, write blog posts, promote your blog, monetize your blog, make money beyond your own blog, and much more. I hope this information helps get you off to a great professional blogging start and well beyond.

Welcome to the blogosphere!

Chapter One
Blogging 101

"You'll always miss 100% of the shots you don't take."
—Wayne Gretzky

As you begin reading this book, you may already know what a blog is. Chances are you have also read quite a few. You may even be an avid follower of several of them. But aside from having some favorite blogs, you may not realize exactly what goes into creating a blog, maintaining it, or even monetizing it. But the truth of the matter is, being a professional blogger is well within your reach, if you want it!

For those who are not so familiar with what a blog is and are interested in leaping into the blogosphere, it is important to get a good idea of what a blog is first. The word *blog* is derived from the phrase "web log," and refers to an online journal that someone creates, usually covering a specific genre or niche topic. The writer, called a blogger, generates posts whenever he or she feels like posting one, which may be daily, weekly, or even several times per day.

Blog posts are typically sorted in chronological order based on when they were posted, or published. Each post is dated, and collectively they create a log. Early blogs were often similar to open online journals, where people would write about various personal topics.

Today there still are plenty of personal journal-type blogs, but there are also blogs covering just about every type of topic, angle, business, and geographic location possible. But don't let that scare you off, because where there's a good blog, there's an audience ready to read it. You just need to create a good blog, which is what you will learn how to do by the time you finish reading this book.

Throughout this book you will come across suggestions for certain activities, like writing about your goals. If you don't already have one, now is a good time to start a blogger's journal, or writer's journal. You don't need anything fancy or expensive. A simple three-ring spiral notebook will do just fine.

A blogger's journal is a good place to jot down all those ideas that come to your mind for blog post topics, but it can also be helpful in answering all the questions that are posed in this book. That way, when you finish reading the book you can look back over the information you logged and you will have done all your homework for getting started—and succeeding—as a professional blogger.

THE DIFFERENCE BETWEEN A BLOG AND A WEBSITE

Many people want to know the difference between a blog and a website. After all, they are both on the Internet, people can visit them, and they both contain content. But if you look more closely, you will see that there are differences between the average blog and website. For starters, blogs typically have dated content that is updated frequently, often on a daily basis. Most websites are created and then the information remains static, which differs from a constantly updated and changing blog.

Additionally, a blog has posts, or articles, which are in reverse chronological order. So the most recent posts are found first, on the home page. When you visit the home page of a blog you know you are usually getting the most updated and fresh content. But it's not like that on a website, as you don't know when the content was placed there, or how long it's been since the site was updated. Additionally, blogs are crawled by search engines more frequently than are most websites. Finally, most blogs allow readers to leave a comment, whereas most websites do not.

ANYONE CAN BLOG

The process to start a blog is easy. *Really* easy. It can be as simple as picking a name and going through a few steps on a screen, answering some basic registration questions along the way. The next step is to add some content, or blog posts, and there you have it! You're in business; you are a blogger.

While this may be true, just going through these steps won't necessarily make you a professional or profitable blogger. There's a lot more to becoming a professional blogger, or one that makes a living from blogging. There are some professional best practices you will need to learn, such as how to set up an attractive blog, write interesting and search-friendly posts, and get the word out about your blog, so that you get plenty of traffic each month.

It is true that anyone *can* blog, but not everyone can be a professional blogger. The only people who make it as professional bloggers are those who really want to. If you want to be a professional blogger, then set your mind to it and make it happen. The only thing standing between you and success is your ability to focus and put your thoughts into action.

You will need to ask yourself what being a professional blogger is to you and what you want to get out of your blogging venture. Some people merely want to blog about their daily adventures in their garden, without any hopes that it ever becomes a popular site, while others want to build the next blog that gets loads of traffic and is widely talked about. You also don't have to choose one or the other, a professional blog and a blog for fun. You can have the best of both worlds and have both types of blogs. There is no limit to the number of blogs you can have, so you can have blogs covering every topic you are interested in. The sky is the limit!

THE HISTORY OF BLOGS

So where did all this blogging stuff begin, anyway? According to *New York* magazine, Justin Hall created the first blog in January of 1994. By December of 1997, the term "Weblog" had been coined for keeping a log on the web.

By August of 1999, the website Blogger had launched a free service that allowed people to create blogs free of charge. The site was a hit and thousands of people began creating blogs. Today, Blogger remains one of the top blogging platform sites, along with Tumblr, WordPress, and Typepad.

There are millions of blogs, millions of bloggers, and millions of others who read blogs. Once blogs came about, people no longer had to rely upon media corporations in order to get information, entertainment, or even the news. Blogs, which are a form of social media, open up the playing field to anyone who wants in on the action. Having said that, it doesn't mean that all blogs are automatically credible and should always be believed or even used as a source.

Many blogs are credible, but as you read them you should always keep in mind that some may not be held to standards that require them to check their facts and cite correct information. This is an issue that will be further explored in chapter five, but you should keep it in mind as you explore blogs and mentally compile the ideas of what it means to be a professional blogger. A professional blogger always aims to provide accurate information.

WHO BLOGS AND WHY?

If you have ever thought about who it is that blogs and why they do it, you are not alone. If you dig a little deeper into the statistics, you will find some interesting insights into who these bloggers are. Nielsen, a company that specializes in gathering information and measuring data, followed 181 million blogs by the end of 2011. The results of their study found that:

- blogging is becoming increasingly popular. Five years prior to this study they had done a similar one that followed 36 million blogs.
- around 6.7 million people (and growing daily) blog through blogging websites, and an additional 12 million people blog using social networking sites.
- the majority of bloggers are women who are well educated. Around 70 percent of bloggers have gone to college, with most earning a degree.
- a third of all bloggers are moms, often called "mommy blog-gers," while 52 percent of all bloggers are parents who have children under the age of eighteen.
- consumer interest in blogs is also increasing, giving bloggers an audience.

This should give you an idea of who blogs, so you can see where you fit in. If you don't fall into any of these categories, it certainly doesn't mean you should walk away from the idea of blogging. Quite the contrary—there's a good chance that you have some-thing unique to bring to the table, giving you an edge over the majority. So have no fear, blog on!

WHY BLOG FOR PROFIT?

A good response to this question is simply, "Why *not* blog for profit?" There is money out there to be made from blogging, and many people in our current economy are struggling to make ends meet. Blogging takes very little money, if any, to get started, making it a venture with a very low investment cost. What you will be investing the most of initially is your time, rather than making the kind of large financial investments that many other small businesses require to get started.

Blogging, for some, is a good source of additional income, but for others it is their main source of financial support. Professional bloggers can make their blogging career what they want it to be—either a part-time gig that brings in some extra spending money, or a full-time career that pays the bills. The choice is yours, depending on what else you are currently doing and what your goals are.

While we are on the topic of blogging for profit, it's important to mention that there are many skeptics out there that believe you can't actually make any money blogging. In short, they are mistaken. Maybe these skeptics have not been successful in their mission to make money by blogging. But there are indeed plenty of people who are succeeding at and profiting from blogging. There are people who, as mentioned, blog to make some extra side money, and still others who have built entire writing careers around being professional bloggers.

MAKING A LIVING

One of the most popular questions when it comes to professional blogging is whether people can actually make a living by doing it. The answer is a resounding "Yes!," you can make a living as a professional blogger. But—yes, there is a "but" in there—you will have to consider a variety of options when it comes to making money from your blogging skills. If you are willing to do that, then you will have a good chance of making a living as a professional blogger.

If, on the other hand, you were to try to make a living only by writing your blog posts, and that's it, nothing more, then the reality is that unless you are getting a heck of a lot of traffic to your site, you may have difficulty earning a living. The good news is that there are quite a few ways that you can monetize your blogging skills, and they all add up to being able to make a living as a professional blogger!

Before you run out and quit your day job to become a professional blogger, you should: a) finish reading this book so you know exactly what you are getting into, and b) consider both sides of the issue. There are two schools of thought when it comes to whether or not you should up and quit your job to become a professional blogger:

Yes, you should quit your job, so that you can give professional blogging your full attention and give it all you've got. This will give you ample time to be productive with blogging, thus increasing your chances of making a living. By not working another job, you will have no excuses and won't feel too tired or burned out from your day job. You will be able to give blogging the attention and dedication that it needs in order for you to succeed.

Now, getting to the point where you can make a living from your blogging skills can take time. This is time that you may not have financially. You have to ask yourself how long you can go not making any income, or making $100 per week, until you get to the point where you have established yourself and can earn a living. To go this route, you would simply work on building a professional blogging career alongside your day job, so that you can establish yourself, get experience, and work your way up to where you are earning a decent salary from your work. This is a route that takes more patience, but may pay off better in the end, as you will be able to ride the waves longer, rather than feeling the pressure to make money to pay the bills right away.

Whether you can afford to quit your job and become a full-time blogger now, or if it's a position you need to gradually move into, is really up to you. Only you know your current financial situation and what you are capable of. There is not one definitive answer that is right or wrong; it's a case-by-case situation. If you have someone else, such as a spouse or partner, that you can rely upon for income as you get started, or if you have money saved up in the bank, you may feel that quitting your job and jumping right in is doable. For those who don't have that financial safety net in place, taking the part-time professional blogging route may be the most attractive. You will still get there. You will just need to be patient, as it may take a little longer.

Speaking of patience, making a living as a professional blogger takes lots of patience for most people. You will need to do everything from starting the blog to building an audience in order to start making money. These things are doable, but you will need to work at it. Blogging is far from a get-rich-quick activity, at least for the majority of people who do it.

It's important to note here that creating a professional blog may open up several routes to earn money. When most people think about the possibility of making money as a blogger, they assume it is just from the articles that they post to their blogs. That may be one route to earning money as a professional blogger, but it certainly isn't the only one. There are quite a few other routes that branch off of that, which you may have not even considered.

Being able to professionally blog is a skill, one that people are willing to pay for, whether through purchasing blog posts, hiring you for blog maintenance, or paying consultation and speaker fees. These additional routes to earning a living as a professional blogger will be explored in chapters nine and ten.

KEEPING POSITIVE

When people create a blog, they take it for granted that it is going to be liked. Maybe it's going to be a small niche topic, so they assume the audience will also be small, or maybe they think that the topic they've chosen has a widespread appeal. Both are perfectly fine, and attainable; it just depends on your goals and what you have in mind.

One great thing about blogging is that it is really something that is open to everyone. No matter what your age, education level, or experience, you can become a professional blogger. All it takes is learning everything you can about your new profession, which is something you are already doing by reading this book, and sticking with it for the long term. There have even been kids who have created popular blogs that get media attention and build a buzz, including those who simply focus on what their school is serving for lunch!

Maintaining a positive attitude is essential to any business venture, or any type of goal that you have in life. When you believe in yourself, your abilities, and your goals, you will be much more successful at achieving them. It's just like Henry Ford once said, "Whether you think you can, or you think you can't—you're right."

Chapter Two
Do You Have What It Takes?

"Knowing yourself is the beginning of all wisdom."
—Aristotle

So you must have an idea that you want to be a blogger, or you wouldn't have made it to this next chapter. Great! But have you thought about why you want to be a blogger? Give that some thought so that you know what you expect to get out of it.

If you want to blog for the sheer love of sharing information on a specific topic, then great, there's not much that you have to worry about in the way of writing blog posts that reach the masses or marketing your blog so that it becomes well known. You can simply set up shop and start writing your blog posts. But if you want to make a living from being a professional blogger, you will need to know more beyond the basics of just setting up the blog and going for it. But don't worry—you will learn the rest of what you need to know throughout this book.

So take a few minutes, or longer, and think about why it is that you want to blog. Do you want to earn some extra money, become an expert on a specific subject, or earn a living? Maybe you want to use your blog to build a platform so that you will have an easier time convincing a publisher that your novel is worthy of a contract and there is an audience waiting to purchase. There is no right or wrong reason for wanting to blog, so don't think that your reason is far-fetched or will get you laughed at. Nobody even has to know why you want to blog, except for you. As long as you know, you will know where you need to go and what you need to do.

Here are some of the reasons that people choose to become bloggers.

- To connect with people who share a common interest. Blogging can be a great way to get in touch with others who share a common passion. For example, perhaps you love Civil War artifacts, or you enjoy nature photography. Having a blog on your favorite topic is an effective way to find others who share your passion. Connecting with others through blogging is common for those who have a passion in a niche area, as well as people who want to be able to connect with others who work in similar industries, especially if they are self-employed.
- To become recognized as an expert in something. Perhaps you want to be known as an expert in making Bundt cakes. Having a blog that covers everything about making Bundt cakes would likely establish you as an expert. While at the outset you may not see how you could make a living from this, you actually could. Thinking bigger, your blog could lead to books, movies, baking lessons, and even Bundt pan endorsements. You just need to think outside of the (cake) box! This is true for much more than making Bundt cakes. You can become an expert in just about anything by establishing a professional blog.
- To share their knowledge with others. Some people know a lot about a particular topic and just want to be able to share it

with others. Creating a blog is a great way to share that information with other people. The information on a blog may be helpful to others in more ways than you realize. For example, if you have a blog that covers a particular medical condition, it may provide a lot of comfort and a great source of information for someone who is going through that particular condition.

- To write. Some people just love to write and a blog gives them an open platform for doing so.
- To promote a company, product, or service. This type of blogging may be done outright, where each post is about the company's products or services, or it may be done by blogging on topics that are closely related to the company's field, in order to bring in readers and eventually convert them to buyers. This type of blog is often used to bring in readers and then direct them to the company's website, where they may be able to purchase products or services.
- To have fun. There are plenty of people who blog just to have some fun. They are likely not taking it too seriously, or looking to earn a living from it, but they find it fun to write the posts and maintain the blog.
- To get free products. There are plenty of people, especially "mommy bloggers," who blog because they want the free products that come with it. Those who are willing to write reviews, in the form of a blog post, can often get a lot of products for free. There are companies that are willing to give bloggers free products in exchange for a review. Depending on what you are blogging about, those products can range from books and dinners out to concert tickets, cameras, or even hotel stays. We will cover full disclosure in chapter nine, because you do need to let your readers know that you were given the products in exchange for a review.

Whether you write to share your passion, to be recognized as an expert, or to make money, these are all valid reasons for blogging. The good news is that, because there are so many reasons that people blog, there is room for all of us. We are not all chasing after the same things or the same sponsors, so there is plenty of room for all of us to have a successful blog, living in harmony in the blogosphere.

WHAT ARE YOUR GOALS AS A BLOGGER?

Now you have a good idea of why people decide to blog. You may have even seen yourself in one or more of the reasons, as well. If you didn't, it's time for you to really get serious about the issue and ask yourself why it is that you want to blog and what your goals are as a blogger.

As a blogger, do you want to:

- make a living?
- find others who share your interest or passion?
- share information on a particular topic?
- establish yourself as an expert in an area?

It's important to know why it is that you want to be a blogger. The clearer the picture in your mind of what you want, the more likely it is you will obtain it. Give some thought to what your goals as a blogger are, so that you know where you are going and if you are making progress toward achieving those goals.

After you get started you will need to establish even more in-depth goals that really narrow down what you want to achieve. For example, you may have a goal of posting at least once per day, finding ten clients to write blog posts for, landing a key sponsor, or getting your monthly traffic up to a certain point. Those are all viable goals to consider once you begin blogging professionally.

Once you have determined your goals as a professional blogger, or what it is that you want to get out of it, then you can work on establishing your additional work goals. To be more successful in achieving all of your blogging-related goals, try to follow the principle of creating S.M.A.R.T. goals, which meet the following criteria.

S – Specific. Your goals should be specific. Try to narrow down the details about what your goal will entail.

M – Measurable. The goals that you set need to be able to be measured in some way, so that you will know if you are making progress toward them.

A – Attainable. Determine how you will achieve the goal. This step gives you a chance to think about what you will need to do in order to attain the result you are looking for.

R – Realistic. Some refer to this step as being *relevant*, rather than *realistic*. But it serves as a reminder that the goal you set needs to be realistic, or relevant, so that you are not setting yourself up for something that wasn't likely to be achieved in the first place.

T – Timely. Hold yourself accountable by narrowing down a time frame. Whether it's three months or six months, it doesn't matter. All that matters is that you set a time frame within which you are going to achieve the goal. You can't leave it open-ended and say "sometime in the future."

The S.M.A.R.T. formula can be used in creating any goals in life. To achieve your professional blogging-related goals, you can use it to set goals for getting your blog started, running the blog once it's up, and maintaining your overall blogging career. It's also a good idea to set some smaller goals throughout your blogging career, so that you make achievements along the way. And don't forget to take the time to celebrate your small accomplishments. Doing so can motivate you to keep reaching for the bigger ones.

Your small goals as a blogger may include things like deciding on a blog topic, registering a domain name, and writing your first post. Your bigger blogging goals may be to create a good revenue stream, get a certain number of subscribers or page views, or have a certain number of blog posts up after one year. Many different small and bigger professional blogging goals are possible. Take some time to think about yours and write them down for future reference. Having an idea floating around in your head and finally getting it on paper can be a wonderful feeling, as well as eye-opening.

HAVING WHAT IT TAKES

Before you take the plunge and get started with blogging, it's a good idea to determine if you have what it takes to be a professional blogger. Not everyone does, and that's fine, but if you want to be a professional blogger you will need to know what it takes, so you can realistically determine if it is something you want to do.

For starters, being a professional blogger means that you will spend a lot of your time writing. Be honest with yourself about how much you enjoy writing. If you enjoy writing and can do it fairly quickly and with ease, then you may love blogging. But on the other hand, if you dread having to sit down and write something longer than your name, blogging may not be the career that you are looking for.

In addition to being able to write, other common skills of a professional blogger include:

- creativity, so that you can continuously come up with blog post ideas
- an understanding of at least basic marketing techniques, so that you can use those skills to promote your blog and get more traffic, page views, and subscribers

- understanding the basic ideas regarding copyright laws, so that you can avoid any plagiarism issue
- knowledge of social media tools that can be used to help build your audience
- the ability and willingness to learn
- patience

You don't need to be a technical person to be able to blog. The one characteristic that is essential is that you are open to learning and will soak up everything that comes your way. There is a lot to learn about blogging, but you can easily learn by reading books like this one and through trial and error once you get started. If you have patience and are willing to stick with the blog, you will learn more all the time and will increase your chances of professional blogging success.

Don't be afraid that you don't know enough about blogging or that you are not technical enough to become a blogger. That's simply not the case with most people. Even those bloggers who have no real technical skills can quickly catch on within weeks or months and be well on their way to using tools, tips, and tricks that can help them with their blogging endeavors. As long as you are willing to keep learning, you will likely do just fine. Besides, even those who are blogging veterans continuously learn the field. They read books and articles and other blogs, attend conferences, take classes, and more. There are always learning opportunities around for those who want to take advantage of them.

TIME AND MONEY

In determining whether or not you have what it takes to become a professional blogger, it's important to touch on the aspects of time and money. Blogging is going to take both of these things, in one way or another, and you need to make sure that you have enough of both of them to get involved comfortably.

17

The time that is involved in blogging will include all of the time that you put into writing blog posts, for your own blog or for a paying client, as well as the time you spend promoting the blog, finding sponsors, responding to emails or comments, interacting with your audience through social media, and even thinking of blog post angles or taking photos for the blog. All of these things may seem small on their own, and it's true that some may take mere minutes, but when you add them all together they will become a decent chunk of time. You need to be sure that you have the time to put into this without straining other areas of your life. The last thing you want is for your marriage or some other close relationships to become strained because you are spending all your free time blogging.

The money that is involved in blogging is minimal, if any at all, in most cases. You can start a blog for free if you want the bare basics, without having your own domain name. Even if you want your own blog name and to use a blogging service that charges, your out-of-pocket expenses for blogging will be minimal. Registering a domain name and signing up with a paid blogging service will cost you less than $100 for the year. Where the money commitment comes into play is that you may lose out on other income as you put in the time to build a successful blog.

For example, let's say you have a job where you get paid by the hour and you decide to cut back a few hours per week so that you can dedicate that time to your blog. Most blogs take some time to get to the point where there is a good return on investment (whether financial or time investment). So the time that you will be putting into building the blog could be costing you. Whatever paid gigs you are giving up during the time you are blogging is the monetary investment that you are making.

Putting in a financial and time commitment should not scare you away from becoming a professional blogger. Not at all! But it is important to mention it, because it's better that you know what you are getting into, so that you can be better prepared for it. Every career out there has such investments, so if you want to become a professional blogger you simply make them, move on, and chalk it up to the investment in your new career. We've all done it, whether some of us realize it yet or not.

QUESTIONS TO ASK YOURSELF

Remember that handy dandy notebook that was suggested to you at the beginning of this book? Hopefully you have been taking notes, answering questions, and writing goals in that book. Doing so will give you a great road map to where you are going with your blogging once you complete this book.

Here is a list of questions to ask yourself about becoming a professional blogger.

1. Do I have the time that is needed to become a professional blogger? This means you will need to commit to blogging at least a few times per week, as well as spending some time marketing your blog.
2. Why do I want to blog and what do I wish to gain from it?
3. Where do I see myself and my blog one year from now, as well as five years from now?
4. What do I think it will take to get there?
5. What three things do I need to do in order to get started?
6. Am I willing to learn all that I can about the field of blogging, so that I know my field and will be more successful?
7. Will I enjoy writing lots of blog posts, or will I feel like it's painful work that I resent?

8. Do I have $100 to invest in registering a domain name and paying for a blogging software service, or do I need to use free services?

9. What am I interested in blogging about? Am I willing to blog on other topics for paying clients?

10. Who is the primary audience for my blog?

Perhaps you don't know the answers yet to all those questions. That's fine. But reading them should get your mental wheels spinning. Remember, the more you think about these questions as you read on, the sooner—and better—you will be prepared to build your blog, get started, and meet your goals.

MY PROFESSIONAL BLOGGING

On a personal note, I have several blogs, all on unrelated topics, but I also earn from writing blog posts for other people and companies. In other words, I do a lot of ghostwriting for blogs, or "ghost blogging." Once you know how to write good blog posts you can sell your service to others. There are plenty of corporations out there that are in need of good professional bloggers. Offering this service is just one more way that you can succeed at earning a living as a professional blogger.

When you "ghostwrite" something, you are exactly that: a ghost in the process. You do the writing, you get paid, but you don't get the recognition or credit for your work. Some people don't care for this, because they like to get recognition for their work. But others, such as myself, don't mind at all, so long as it helps pay the bills at the end of the month. If someone is willing to pay me to write blog posts, I have no problem with my name not being attached to them, or with my not being able to use them as examples of my writing. After all, both the company and I know that I wrote them, and my bank account has confirmed it. I've ghostwritten blog posts (as well as books) for many corporations and some big-name people in various industries, but I respect the fact that it's ghostwriting and never make my authorship known to others. It's important to note that as a professional, any time you are hired to ghost-write blog posts for others it is unethical for you to share with others the fact that you wrote them. When it comes to ghostwriting, mum's the word!

One of my blogs, VolusiaCountyMoms.com, is a local site for families to find information on events and things to do within our area, which happens to be the Daytona Beach area. I put a lot of thought into it before delving in and creating this blog. I knew I wanted to reach local families, cover events, feature pictures of local places, and even have an events calendar of family-friendly things to do. In November of 2009 I launched the site and since then it has been steadily growing. I now have a large number of blog posts, page views per month, and paid advertisers, and my blog continues to grow in each of these areas.

Part of what made my blog successful is that I knew what I wanted to do with it, I knew how I was going to do it, and then I dove right in. Having a vision of what you want, what you want to do with it, and where you want it to go can help ensure that your blog will be successful—whether on a local, national, or global scale.

A BLOG THAT FAILS

It may seem as though the pressure is on to figure out everything about the blog now so that it's successful. But it's really not like that. You can kill a blog, or end it, just as easily as you can create one. Part of the beauty in it being so easy to start blogs is that you can be a serial blogger, having several blogs on various topics. You will have the ability to see which blogs do well and which ones can't seem to get off the ground. Those that don't get off the ground, you can either give them a lift, or you can ditch them and move on to another blog idea. There are people, even companies, who practice serial blogging, trying many ideas and keeping those that do well, and ditching the ones that don't.

The bottom line is that maybe your first blog will be a bust, or maybe your fourth one will be, but that's fine; just keep going. You are going to find that some of your blogs will resonate with readers and others will not, and you are not bound to having just one blog or to covering one genre. You are free to spread your wings, blog as much as you want, create as many blogs as you want, and see what works and what doesn't. If you find you have a blog that can't get off the ground and you are going to ditch it, use it as a learning experience. Try to determine why it wasn't successful, so that you can avoid repeating that with your next blog.

We will get into serial blogging in chapter eleven, but know that it is an option. It's a great way to help you in your quest for earning a living as a professional blogger. Keep the idea of serial blogging in mind as you go along. As you take notes and jot down ideas about what you'd be interested in blogging about, you may find you are interested in several ideas or genres. Happily, you don't have to pick just one and ax the others. You can try them all and see which you like in reality more than theory and which ones seem to quickly find an audience. Think of it as throwing spaghetti against the wall and seeing what sticks! Try several blogs and you are bound to have some that stick (or become successful).

SUCCESSFUL BLOGGERS (AND WHY THEY ARE)

You may be wondering what it is exactly that makes for a successful blog. You are not alone! Every person who engages in blogging, and even some who don't, wants to know what makes some bloggers more successful than others. Is it the topic's mass appeal? The writing style? There is no sure-fire formula for being a successful blogger. There are some things that make blogs, and thereby bloggers, more successful than others, though.

It's a good idea to spend a little time looking over successful blogs, so that you can see for yourself what it is that you think helps to make them successful. As you look at the site, notice their content, ads, pictures, or anything else that stands out. See if you can determine what they are doing to promote their site (e.g., social media, advertising, etc.), and if they are doing anything else to increase their revenue on their blog (e.g., offering writing services, consulting services, or selling products, etc.). By studying a few of the top bloggers out there you may be able to pick up a few pointers that can be helpful in creating your own blog.

SUCCESSFUL BLOGGERS (AND WHO THEY ARE)

If you do a search to come up with the most successful bloggers, or blogs, you are sure to find a dizzying list of suggestions. There are quite a few different types of lists out there that that suggest the "top" blogs or bloggers. But all these lists seem to focus on different variables. Some may be ranking the best based on traffic, while others may be putting together a list of their personal favorites. Therefore it's a little difficult to pick what the top blogs are. Perhaps you have your own personal list of top blogs and bloggers; it just depends on what your criteria for judging each happens to be.

Having said that, there are some blogs that I believe should be mentioned, simply because they are so popular. Look over this list of blogs and then take a few minutes to personally check out each one. These blogs are well known and the bloggers have made a successful mark in the field. See what you like, or don't like, about what they have done with their blogs.

Ten successful blogs to check out and study (in no particular order):

1. **HuffingtonPost.com**—Not only did Arianna Huffington create a popular news-filled blog, featuring many different authors, but the site also makes a lot of money. At one time it was reported to be making around $2.3 million per month in advertising revenue. But what's more, in 2011 she sold the site to AOL for a cool $315 million. Keep in mind, however, that she started the site with a $1 million investment.

2. **ZenHabits.net**—With over 250,000 subscribers, this blog has reached success largely by word of mouth. Rather than advertising on the site, earnings are made through ancillary products, such as books and online courses (more to come on that in chapter nine).

3. **Mashable.com.**—This site focuses on technology, digital trends, and social media. Many bloggers use it as a way to keep up on what's new in the world of blogging. The site gets 20 million unique visitors per month.

4. **Copyblogger.com**—Started in 2006, this blog offers tips and tricks for bloggers, and other website authors, on how to have more valuable content and get the most out of your efforts.

5. **TreeHugger.com**—A Discovery Company blog, this one focuses on all things environmental. Those who want to know about everything from recycling to solar laptops visit this blog to find out what's new in being green.

6. **ChrisGuillebeau.com**—Chris offers a popular blog called the *Art of Non-Conformity*, where he offers advice on personal growth, entrepreneurship, and thoughts on changing the world. He also chronicles his world travels, and offers books and courses as additional sources of revenue.

7. **TechCrunch.com**—Founded in 2005, this site focuses on technology and gets around 37 million page views per month. Additional revenue sources include the major conferences and events that it hosts.

8. **SethGodin.typepad.com**—This is a popular blog for those seeking business and entrepreneurial information, tips, and advice. Being a successful book author, Seth uses his blog as a platform for keeping in touch with, and continuing to provide information to, his followers. Additionally, Seth founded the popular site Squidoo.com.

9. **TMZ.com**—People are obsessed with celebrities and want to know their every move. That obsession has helped propel the TMZ blog to popularity, which means they get a lot of traffic each month.

10. **DrudgeReport.com**—This site became widely known for first putting out rumors about the 1998 Lewinsky scandal. Today the site still gets a lot of traffic as people like to see what other stories may break on the site.

As you can see, these popular blogs have varied themes. While some focus on environmental issues, others publish celebrity gossip, and others focus on technology. There are many possibilities when it comes to finding a good blog topic to cover, because the world is made up of billions of people who are all seeking different information. Additionally, as you look over those sites you will notice various layout styles, as well as revenue streams beyond straight site advertising.

Chapter Three
Choosing Your Focus

"Passion rebuilds the world for the youth. It makes all things alive and significant."
—**Ralph Waldo Emerson**

One of the hardest questions for people to answer is, "What should I blog about?" It seems like it would be a pretty straightforward decision, but that's not always the case. Choosing what to create a blog about, for many people, can be a challenge. If it seems that finding a blog focus is difficult it could be because you are going about it wrong, or simply putting too much thought into it. At times, we can overanalyze something, making it much more difficult than it needs to be.

If you already know what you want to blog about, great! But if you are like most people who are just getting started, you probably have several ideas floating around in your head and are not sure what your focus will be. Or maybe you have an idea, but you question how viable it is. After reading this chapter you will be well on your way to knowing what you would like to blog about, even if you have multiple topic areas.

DECIDING WHAT TO BLOG ABOUT

So you know you want to blog, yet you aren't sure what you want to blog about? Don't worry, you are not alone! Remember that this is a short-term problem. Determining what you will blog about is much simpler than you may think it is. Pull out your handy dandy notebook, because there are a few things you can do to help come up with the ideal blog angle to get started.

For starters, consider what type of blogs you tend to like. Do you have blogs that you read regularly or subscribe to? Notice if there is a common theme among them. Take note of that theme in your notebook. It could help you identify an area that you are passionate about, and as we will learn, having passion for a topic will carry you a long way.

Beyond looking at the types of blogs that you like to read, consider as well the type of books and magazines you enjoy. Usually there is a common theme among such media items, and they create a strong blueprint for the types of topics that you are really interested in. Blogging requires writing a great deal about a particular topic, so it really helps if it's an area that interests you a lot as well.

MAKING A LIST, CHECKING IT TWICE

While you have your notebook ready, another good way to drum up blog ideas is to start making a list. Make a list of:

- things you have experience with. This includes your jobs, hobbies, volunteering, coaching, etc. Anything you have had a decent amount of experience at should go on the list.
- things that you really enjoy doing, such as traveling, nature photography, surfing, or skiing. Whatever it is that you enjoy doing, get it down on the list.
- things that you are good at. That doesn't mean you have to have had special training at it or that you particularly love it,

at this point, just get it all down on the list. If you just so happen to be good at baking birthday cakes, for example, put it down on the list.

- topics you would choose if there were no limits and you could not fail at being successful. In other words, what type of blog would you have if you absolutely knew you could not fail at it?

- things that you would like to help others with. Perhaps you know a lot about childcare, divorce, or caring for elderly parents. Many people could be helped by reading such information, and they are all ideas that should be listed.

- subjects that you tend to read about. Whether it is online articles, magazine articles, or books, see if there's a pattern to what you like to read. Also include the themes of any blogs that you currently read or follow.

- topics you would blog about if you knew you could not fail. Describe your dream successful blog. Be bold, be brave, and write down what it is that you would successfully blog about if success was guaranteed.

Once you are done jotting down these ideas, take a look at the list. It doesn't have to be immediately; you can even wait a few hours or a full day. But when you are ready, go back to the list and look for common themes and those topics that really seem to get you excited. Notice if your creative juices start flowing with a particular idea or two.

Try to narrow your list down to three to five ideas that you are the most excited by or interested in blogging about. From there, you can narrow it down more to determine which one you want to get started with—but don't ditch the other ideas altogether. As discussed previously, and it will be explored further in chapter ten, serial blogging is a real possibility, so you may want to have those ideas for a later time. Serial blogging is great, and will help to increase your earnings potential, but it's best to get started with one topic at a time. Once you get one blog off the ground, then you can start working on other ones. But for now, we need to narrow the focus for your first blog.

NARROWING YOUR TOPIC

While there may be some blogs out there that can get away with being eclectic and actually be successful while doing it, most tend to narrow it to a general topic or theme. For example, the Huffington Post, which was mentioned earlier for being one of the most popular blogs around, does not stick to one topic. However, the theme is that it is a news site, so you can expect that a wide variety of news topics will be covered.

Whether you focus on something specific, such as hiking through the Appalachian Mountains, or something broad, such as hiking across America, it is important to know what the focus of your blog is going to be. How narrowly you focus it, or how broad your appeal is, is totally up to you. But even a broad appeal will generally have a common theme or connection.

If you want to make a living from blogging, you may have to focus more on demand, rather than just writing about what you love. That's not to say that you cannot make a living blogging about what you love, but it really depends on what the topic is. Let's say you have a passion for heirloom tomatoes, or the skink (a type of lizard). You may be passionate about your topic, but that doesn't necessarily mean there is enough demand, or traffic, to help get you to the point where you can make a living from it.

At the same time, if you do have a highly focused topic, that doesn't mean that you *can't* make a living writing about it. If you are willing to use your blog as a springboard for making money from the topic in other ways, there is a good chance you can still make a living from it. This really comes down to your approach, and what you are willing to do to make it work.

It's important to keep in mind that if you plan to make a living from your blogging, you will need to think of it as a business, because it *is* a business. When someone opens a business they first need to determine that there is enough demand for the product they are going to offer. Then they have to treat it like a business, so that they can focus on earning. Having a blogging business is really no different. Think of it as a business, treat it like a business, and there's a better chance your blog will be one of the successful ones.

EVALUATING YOUR PASSIONS

The best way to start narrowing your blog theme is to sit down and brainstorm a list of everything you would be interested in blogging about. You already have a list of the questions to ask yourself and what should be included. Once you have answered all these questions, you can spend some time going over the list. You will likely find some common themes. Highlight those topics that get you the most excited, so you can consider those first.

After you have this list, and have highlighted the ones you are most interested in, start doing a little research to see if the demand is there for such topics. Demand shouldn't be your sole reason for or against choosing a blog topic, but it is important to consider it, if you want to have a successful blog.

Take one topic at a time and do some online searches to find similar sites that cover the topic. When you have found a few, and have checked them out, log onto Alexa.com to see what their traffic is like. Alexa.com will give you a look at the traffic to every site on the Internet. Just plug in the name of the site and you will have the information you need to see if the site is getting any traffic. Keep in

31

mind that the lower the Alexa ranking, the better. In other words, a site ranked at 1.4 million is getting a lot more traffic than a site ranked at 14 million, and so on. The lower the rank, the more traffic the site is getting on a regular basis.

Sometimes Alexa will show the global ranking, as well as the site rank for the United States. While it always provides the global ranking, if the site has been picked up by Alexa and is getting enough traffic to be included, then it doesn't always show the U.S. ranking.

Using Alexa is a helpful way to gauge the demand, or interest that people have in a particular topic. It will help you see how successful other bloggers are at bringing in traffic to sites that may have similar topics to the ones you are considering. However, that doesn't mean you can't do better than theirs. Some bloggers are better at bringing in traffic, writing blog posts, and engaging their audience. So while the numbers give you an idea of the demand, they don't tell the whole story.

After you have taken a look at the Alexa ranking, there's another tool that you can use to gauge demand for the topic. That insightful tool is the Google AdWords Keyword Tool. You can find it by doing a quick Google search for it, or by logging onto https://AdWords.google.com. All you need to do is type in a topic and see what kind of results it shows.

Let's say you are interested in blogging about the fast food industry. Using the AdWords tool, type "fast food industry" into the search field and conduct a search. The results will show both the local monthly Google searches for that term, as well as the global monthly searches for the term. This will give you a chance to see how often people are searching for the topic you are considering, and it will also give you a chance to consider other similar topics and angles. Take a look at the list of additional words it pulls up to see if anything that catches your eye gets a lot of searches. If so, add it to your list!

In addition to the Google AdWords tool there are other options. Wordtracker is online software that will give you keyword information. While the Google tool is free to use, WordTracker does have a monthly or yearly fee for using it as much as you like. You will need to decide whether it is an investment worth making. The site does offer a money-back guarantee, so you can use it for a month and if you find you are not happy with it you can get your money back.

EVALUATING YOUR LIST

Hopefully when you wrote your list of blog theme ideas you came up with at least fifty of them. The more topics you added to the list, the better, so that you have more options to consider. While it may take some time to evaluate the demand for each topic on your whole list, it's well worth the effort. The more you can evaluate the topic and know what to expect, the better position you will be to choose a topic that will give you the level of income opportunities you are seeking.

As you evaluate your list of ideas by looking over other sites covering those topics, checking their Alexa ranking, and seeing how many Google searches there are each month for the topic, you should get a good picture of each topic. You may even start highlighting particular topics as being more probable of having success, or you may start crossing some ideas off as you see that there is not a lot of demand or interest in the topic.

Try to narrow down your topics to two or three ideas that you would enjoy writing about on a regular basis, and that you think have the potential for getting a lot of traffic. While you will choose one to begin with, we will explore serial blogging later on in chapter ten, so you can always add the other two blogs at a later time.

MARKET OVERSATURATION

One thing you may come across as you conduct research is that certain topics seem oversaturated. Perhaps you have a popular blog topic that interests you, such as entrepreneurship, and there are many blogs and sites covering the topic. Just because the market may seem to be widely covered on the topic, that doesn't mean you should automatically move onto another idea.

Some topics may have enough room in the market to support another site, especially if the Google search tool shows that a lot of people are searching for that particular topic each month. Even if you start a blog covering a topic in a sea of similar topics, you can still differentiate yourself and gain an audience. There are ways you can do that, such as building a relationship with your audience, and other ways we will look at in chapters six and twelve.

The blog topic you choose is not set in stone either, so don't think you have to pick something that you will be stuck with forever. You can always change your blog topic later, or you can delete that blog and start a new one. There are many options available to you. Many people think about starting a blog, but are too afraid to commit to a topic. It's better to pick a topic that you may end up changing or tweaking later on, than it is to sit idle, not getting the blog started at all.

On another note, it's helpful if the topic you choose is something that you do have some experience with. If you have work experience, education, or volunteer work, it will help to establish you as an expert. But don't let that stop you from starting a blog on a topic that you are not already an expert in or have a lot of experience with. You can learn as you go along and share that experience with your readers. In the field of writing there is an old adage that people should "write what they know." While I think that is a safety net, it doesn't allow a lot of room for growth as a writer. It boxes you in and prevents you from learning about new things and making money by writing things you may not know much about at all.

Unlike the "write what you know" advice you may get elsewhere, I believe that you should write what you are interested in, what you want to learn about, and what will help pay your bills. There can be a lot of different motivating factors behind why you write about what you write about. And that's okay! Write what you know if you happen to be an expert in it and want to spend a lot of time writing about it. But don't let that old saying keep you from spreading your wings and taking a chance on your dream topic.

On a routine basis I write blog posts for my own blogs as well as for a variety of other clients. I have a list of clients who pay me to write blog posts for them, mainly in a ghostwriting capacity. There's no way that I could "know" about all the topics that I write blog posts about. Not even close. But every good writer must be a good researcher, so if you can research a topic, and learn about it, then you can write about it as well. Including work outside of what you know, or outside your comfort zone, can give you a chance to make more money as a professional blogger.

After conducting all the necessary plotting and researching to determine the best blog topic to go with it, it's time to gets started and turn your ideas into blog posts!

Chapter Four
Getting Started

*"The secret of getting ahead is getting started. The secret
of getting started is breaking your complex overwhelming tasks
into small manageable tasks, and then starting on the first one."*
—**Mark Twain**

Once you have decided what to blog about, it's time to get started. This is where it gets exciting, or for some people, a little confusing and scary. Even if you are completely new to blogging and have absolutely no technical abilities, you don't need to fear blogging. The act of blogging is quite simple, at least as far as setting up the blog itself. For some people, the more challenging aspect is in the writing of the post and coming up with ideas for posts.

CHOOSING YOUR BLOG NAME

One of the most important things that you will need to do first is to create a blog name. For some people this comes to them easily, but for others it can be a daunting task. I'm a fan of the brainstorming method when trying to figure out something like this, so I would recommend using your notebook to compile a list of possible names.

As you begin to write possible blog titles, ideas will probably start flooding to you, at least for a little while.

Just jot down all the names, even if you think they may not be good. The best thing to do is get down as many potential titles as possible. Get creative and think of different ways to say things or play on word phrases. If you have a thesaurus handy, use that to see what alternate words you can come up with for words you are considering.

Having a good blog name is important. It will help people to make a connection with your blog, get to know it, and help give your blog its own unique identity. Your blog name may give clues about what your blog is about as well. Here are some tips for choosing your blog name.

- Choose a name that you really like. Don't just settle for something to pick a name quickly. If waiting an extra day or week is going to help you find a great name, then be patient and wait it out. This is a blog name that you will hopefully have for years to come, so it's better to wait until you have what you think is the perfect name, providing that wait doesn't become an excuse that keeps you from getting started.

- Try to choose a blog title that is going to give you a little room for what you will write about. If you want to write about entrepreneurialism, choose a name that will allow you to write on a variety of related topics. If you were to choose the title, "Your First Week in Business," then you would run out of things to write about pretty quickly. A really narrowly focused blog title may prevent you from spreading out a little and comfortably covering the whole topic. Go a little more general, rather than narrowly focused.

- If possible, and it is usually possible, try to think of a name that is on the shorter side and is easy to remember. Longer names will not only be more difficult to find a domain name for, but will also be harder for readers to remember and type in. Keep it short and simple, if possible.

- Try to make sure the name gives readers a clue about what they will find being covered at your blog. Some people may get away with using their own name, especially if they are a writer who is promoting their books. But if what you are doing is not directly promoting your name, tie the name of the blog to what it is that you are promoting or are blogging about.

- Whatever name you pick, the matching domain name really needs to be available. This can be a hurdle, because so many domain names are already registered. But it's really important that your blog name match your title. If you are set on having a blog name that doesn't match the domain, try to keep the domain name a shorter version of the blog name. For example, if your blog is "Business Start-up Coaching," go with something like "startupcoaching" for the domain name, assuming it's available. This makes it easier for people to remember and find you.

- While it's not completely necessary, it can be helpful if your blog title also includes some keywords that can be used to help bring traffic into your site. For example, if your blog is focused on Hawaii, it would be ideal to include the term Hawaii in the title.

- Try to steer clear of words that will be difficult for people to spell. If they are trying to type in your blog name or do a search for it and can't remember how to spell it, they may just move on to reading something else.

One of my blogs, which was started in November 2009, is a local site for families. I didn't feel there was a good family-oriented site in the area that provided family-friendly events and information. I spent some time brainstorming what I wanted to call it, what parts of the county I wanted to cover, and what keywords I should use. In the end, I settled upon the name Volusia County Moms.

While there were more people searching for the term "Daytona Beach" each month, I decided upon "Volusia County" for a couple of reasons, including the fact that those searching for Daytona Beach are often visitors to the area. While I appreciate the visitors stopping by the site, they really weren't my intended target audience. Visitors would come to the site to find local information for a specific trip, but then wouldn't be regular users of it. However, the people I was trying to reach, moms who lived in the county, would most likely find the site, and by sticking with "Volusia County" I included the whole county, rather than narrowing it to one city within it.

The name that I chose is one that shows the blog covers the whole county, and is geared toward moms. Once they log on they can see that the site offers family-friendly information for those who live in the county. Those visiting may find some of it of interest, but the target audience is moms living in the county, who may be looking for things to do with their children, local business reviews, parenting information, and so on.

FINDING A URL

Every blog needs to have a URL, which stands for uniform resource locator. Basically, the URL is the web address where your blog is found. You have a couple of options, depending on where you host your blog. For example, if you choose to go with Blogger.com, you have the ability to create a name within their family. If you were to have a blog titled "Little Red Car," then you could have a URL like littleredcar.blogger.com, or you have the ability to go with your own unique URL. If littleredcar.com was available, you could use that.

Finding a URL can certainly be a task. Log into a site like Network Solutions and test out some ideas to see what is available. This will allow you to try the ideas you have, as well as providing you with some closely related alternate options if the one you want is already taken. This is a process that can go on for hours as you try different combinations, until you finally find one that you like that is available.

Let's look at a few of the common top-level URL extensions and what they mean. As you are researching URL possibilities you will be offered .com, .org, .net, .us, and various others. Here's what the various options are typically used for.

.com—This is a commercial domain name that anyone can use and is the most popular option in America.

.biz—This is a domain extension that was designed to be used by businesses.

.info—This is an option that anyone can register and will often be used by information-related sites, or by sales sites where people may log on to find more about a product or service.

.mobi—This extension is for those sites that have been designed to be mobile device compatible.

.name—The extension is used by people to register their name as the domain name. You do not need to use this to register your name, you can use the other extensions as well, but it's an option.

.org—This extension is for organizations and is often used by non-profit and for-profit entities.

.net—This is a network option and is usually used by larger sites that may have smaller sites within it.

.xxx—This is an extension that relates to pornography. If you have a blog that will include pornography this may be an option you'll want to consider.

.us—This is a country code extension that stands for the United States. Other countries have their own extension code, such as .ca for Canada.

This is only a partial list of the various domain extensions available to you. There are others, including country extensions, that are also available. You will also find that there are ones that are not available to you, such as .edu (education-related sites), .gov (government sites), and .mil (military sites). So which option should you go with when choosing one? Here are a few tips for choosing your domain name and extension.

- Avoid registering any names that may be mistaken for another company, especially one that is large and will likely come knocking on your door later to take it back from you. For example, even if you can register something like HersheyChocolate.com, you may as well avoid it. The company can prove that the name is theirs and will likely be able to take it from you if they want to.

- Try to get the .com extension name if at all possible. The .com extension is the one that most people are familiar with and is the easiest to remember. Even if you do register a .us there is a good chance that when people type in the web address they will mistakenly put a .com on the end of your URL, out of habit. Think for a moment how many non-.com names you type in each week and you will see how rare it is that you purposely visit sites that do not end in .com—so keep it simple. If the .com is not available, and you feel that is the best possible name for your blog, then move on to considering other extension options.

- You will likely come across a lot of advice telling you to purchase most of the extensions of the name you go with. If you have money to burn, go for it. But in most cases this is simply not necessary for a blogger. Snatching up every name combination, including misspellings, may be something that large corporations want to do, but as a blogger it's not necessary.

- There's nothing wrong with using your own name as your blog URL. If you go this route, try to register your first/last name and the .com version.

- Avoid putting dashes or hyphens in your domain name. While they may help with spacing out the title or with SEO (Search Engine Optimization, which refers to using search engine–friendly keywords), people will rarely remember them when typing in the address.

- Try to keep the name as short as possible. The longer your domain name is, the harder it will be for people to remember it, and the more opportunity they have for spelling errors while typing it in.

- If you have the extra money, purchase the domain name for a longer period of time, rather than just paying for one year up front. Going for several years will knock money off the yearly fee and you won't have to worry about renewing it each year.

At this point you may be wondering if it is better to use the blogging-service domain, such as the .blogger.com example, or to use your own domain name. Without a doubt it is better to use your own domain name. They are inexpensive, easier to remember, and much easier to brand and promote. Having a long URL, including adding in something like the .blogger name, will just make it more difficult for people to remember your domain name. Keep your blog domain name as short as possible, simple, easy to remember, and uniquely yours.

PUBLISHING YOUR BLOG

Once you have decided on a URL for your blog, it's time to make a decision about how you will go about publishing it. There are a lot of decisions to make when first setting up your blog, but the good news is that once they are in place you won't have to worry about those things anymore, for the most part.

There are many options for hosting your blog. Even social networks like Facebook and MySpace are set up to allow you to create posts and send them out to your followers. While some people do take that option, most people tend to go with a dedicated blogging publisher. There are quite a few options when it comes to choosing a publishing tool as well. Take the time to research each one so that you can decide which is the right choice for you. It's much easier to start off using the publishing site you want to use, rather than wanting to change or move it later on.

One of the nice things about blogging is that you don't actually have to know HTML (hypertext markup language). While some people may choose to write their blog posts using HTML, there are plenty of web-based publishing options that will help you avoid it if you'd prefer to. While I've taken an HTML class, I'd much prefer to write my blog posts avoiding it if possible. That doesn't mean you don't need to have any web or technical skills at all. Just publishing a blog doesn't take any of those skills, because the publishers available today are straightforward and easy to use. However, to publish a good blog that is interactive and will engage your readers will likely require that you take the time to learn a few things. Whether you want to add widgets, plug-ins, or events calendars, they are a little more advanced than just writing a post and hitting the "publish" key.

The good news is that these things can easily be learned by someone willing to put a little time in to gain the skills.

Here are some of the more common blogging hosting options that are available online today.

- **Typepad.** This popular blogging site is not free; however, the fee you pay per year for blogging is minimal. For around $10 per month you can use their software to create and manage your blog, which will also allow you to choose your design and layout, add typelists (custom boxes), and more. Depending on the price level you want to pay, and how many blogs you would like to maintain, you can even go for the option that allows you to have an unlimited number of blogs for one monthly fee. Even for their lowest monthly option you can have four blogs for the one fee. Since 2009, Typepad is the service that I have used for my blogs, so I am most familiar with it, although I have used several others on behalf of my clients. I have found it easy to work with and have been happy with the service.

- **Blogger.** Many people choose Blogger, owned by Google, simply because they make it easy to set up their ads on the site. It's also a well-known name in the blog publishing field. However, setting up ads on other blogging publisher tools is not difficult, so don't base your whole decision on the fact that Blogger is owned by Google. My Google ads were not difficult to set up on my blogs, even though I don't use Blogger. One of the most attractive features of using Blogger is that it's free. So you can do all your blogging and not pay for the space.

- **WordPress.** This is another of the more popular blog publishing routes. They do offer a free option, which is limited in storage space, as well as a premium upgrade package you can pay for. With WordPress you can buy extra storage as you need it, adding on anywhere from 3 to 200 extra GB of storage space for a fee. You can also opt to upgrade to being able to custom design your site, and more. With à la carte options, you have the ability to pick and choose which upgrades you want to spring for and which you would rather pass on.

These are just a few of the many blog publishing sites that are available today. There are many more options, including Squarespace, xanga, and LiveJournal. You also have the ability to blog using MySpace, AOL, and a variety of other sites. Nearly all of these tools will give you the option of using HTML or not, as well as using a template to design your site.

So just how do you go about choosing which one you want to use? Well, you can ask around to see what others use, but you will always get advice that will be partial to the one that they use. That doesn't necessarily mean it will be the option you are the happiest with. Before starting your blog, visit some blog publishing sites and read them over. Determine what it is that you want out of a blog publishing tool, or host, such as whether you want a free service, one that you pay a flat fee for unlimited space, or one that you pay for additions as you need them. There are people that use each of these services. While there may be some people who are unhappy with them, there are many more who are happy with the publisher they are using. It's just a matter of deciding which one is the right one for you. Avoid starting the blog until you have researched hosts and made a decision on which will be the best. It's easier to do that than try to move it later on.

Each of the blogging hosts will likely have pricing options that range from free to a couple of hundred dollars per year. But that price range will be impacted by the storage space you need, if you want a custom domain name, and whether or not you want to have one blog or one hundred. Keep these points in the back of your mind as you are making your comparisons.

DESIGNING YOUR BLOG

Looking at other people's blogs, you will see that there are quite a few options when it comes to design. Some people have custom designs, while others go with a template. The easiest option is to sift through the templates available at the publishing company you decide to use. If you are a technical person, or someone who does graphics work, then you may want to opt for a custom look.

Templates are ease to use, because you simply find one you like the look of and select it. That's it! The work has all been done for you. Once you've selected your template you can plug in your information and extras into the spots on the blog. Templates will likely give you options of having one, two, and three columns. You can see what other sites look like that have these columns. They usually have the content going down the middle of the page, with ads and links running down both sides of the blog page. Look at the options and decide which is going to be the most ideal for you and what you have in mind for your blog.

If you are a graphic person you will most likely not want to go with a template. That's understandable and I would encourage you to create your own unique image using your skills. When I speak about the use of templates I'm referring to those people, including myself, who are not graphically or technically inclined, and need something that is super simple and can be set up with minimal effort. I use templates, rather than anything uniquely designed, because it's easy and affordable.

When you are setting up your blog look and design, keep in mind that most people will be reading "above the fold," which means that they will see what is on the screen, without having to scroll down in order to see more. Also, the font style and overall blog colors that you use matter in keeping people reading and it being visually appealing. Blogs are typically set up in a two- or three-column format. You will have the ability to preview the options to see which one you like better. If you plan ahead of time what you want to have on your blog (e.g., ads, search box, calendar, etc.), you can take that into consideration when choosing which layout you would like to use. But don't feel like you are stuck with that layout, or that it has to be a lasting decision. You can always change it at a later time. It's easy to change the layout and within minutes you can usually have a whole new look.

When it comes to what people will be reading on your blog, opt for fonts that will be compatible with different Internet browsers and easy on the eyes. If you aren't sure which ones are easy to read, have a few people read your posts in the font you are considering, and ask for their feedback on the font. There are a few blogs I've been to that have colors and fonts that are so difficult to take in that I can't wait to leave the page. You don't want your readers, or anyone that stumbles across your pages, to be thinking that same thing. Black sites with scary fonts may seem like a cool idea at the outset, but unless the blog is focused on Halloween fright night, these themes could get old quickly and could negate some of your blog promotion efforts.

Color helps to set the tone or mood of a blog, so you want to choose one that is going to help establish your brand and identity. Color psychology, the impact that color has on people, is a well-documented issue and something you want to take into consideration. For example, blue is a common color used for businesses because it is believed to help build trust, while red can elicit strong emotions in people, such as excitement or passion. When designing your blog, take a moment to think about the colors you will use and what feelings they may bring about in your readers. You want to make sure that the feelings associated with the colors you choose coincide, rather than conflict, with your mission.

ESTABLISHING YOUR BRAND

In designing your blog you will be establishing your brand, or image. Take some time to think about what you want your brand and image to be, then work it into your plan to make it happen. What people see when they visit your blog is a representation of your brand, whether it's for yourself or for a company you are blogging for. Make sure that the design you choose, including layout, color, and fonts, are sending the message you intend.

Chapter Five
Writing Blog Posts

"The writer must write what he has to say, not speak it."
—Ernest Hemingway

Becoming a professional blogger means that you will be spending a lot of your time writing. This is something you have to make sure you are comfortable with. Since you are reading this book, let's assume that you already realize that blogging takes a great deal of writing, and that you have some sort of writing ability, which has prompted you to consider this field. Those who feel they could use some additional experience in this area can get it in a variety of ways, such as taking a writing course at a local community college, taking an online writing course, reading books about the writing process, or simply practicing daily. Joining a local writer's group that offers critiques can also be helpful in honing your writing skills.

When it comes to being good at writing blog posts, it is really a matter of experience. The more you do it, the better you will tend to get. It's like that with all things in life. If you learn more about what goes into blog posts, what makes for an interesting blog post, and how to write one that will keep your reader interested, then you will be just fine. You don't have to enter the field knowing all the answers about how to create the perfect blog post. You just need to be able to learn, practice, and repeat. Your posts will get better in time and you will learn more as you continue blogging.

By now you should be ready to take on writing your first blog posts, and get started drawing traffic into your site. Some people tend to get a little nervous at this point, but you shouldn't. That's what the blog is all about—sharing what you know, getting readers to visit, and interacting with your audience.

WRITING YOUR FIRST POST

You may already have something in mind that you want your first post to cover. But it's a good idea to start out with a post that describes who you are and what your blog is about. This is a good chance to give people a snapshot of what they can expect from your blog.

Things to cover in the first blog post include:

- **an introduction.** A blog is a social media tool, so be social. Engage with the readers (or potential readers, since you may not have any steady readers yet). Introduce yourself, so they know who you are. If you have any special training, education, or experience in this area be sure to share that with them, so you begin to establish yourself as an expert on the topic you will be writing about.
- **a description.** Give the reader an overview of what your blog is going to be about. Provide an idea of the topics and issues that will be covered, as well as how you came about wanting to cover this topic. Let them know what to expect by reading your blog.
- **an explanation of what you're trying to accomplish.** Tell the reader in this first post why it is that you are creating this blog. Do you want to share knowledge, build a community, or something else? Let them know what has motivated you to

pick the particular topic you are covering. Also, explain why they will want to come back to your blog again. What's in it for them? Will they be able to learn, share stories, get ideas, be inspired, or what? People always want to know what they will get out of something.

- **an invitation to readers to follow you and your blog.** In this first post, ask your reader to stay tuned for more posts and to check out your blog again. Invite them to sign up to receive your blog posts via email or feed, and/or to follow you on Twitter and Facebook. Include the links in your post for them to do that, so they don't have to go hunting for them. The easier you make it for them to sign up to follow your blog, the more likely they will do it.

- **a definition of your audience.** Let the readers know who the blog is intended for. If you are trying to reach middle-aged bald men around the country, or just in Idaho, be sure to write that. While some blogs may have a wide audience range, most can narrow down whom their blog is for. Examples of this include, "This blog is for everyone who wants to learn all about the frogs that inhabit Maine," or, "This blog is for anyone who wants to keep up on the latest techie toys that hit the market."

- **contact information.** Let your readers know that they can feel free to contact you, or leave comments. Since blogs are social forums, you may start out by allowing comments, but if your blog gets big and has a lot of traffic, or if it gets to a point where you get a lot of spam advertising, you may need to revise your policy on communication. We will explore this topic further in chapter seven.

This is just a suggested guideline for what to include in your first blog post. There's nothing written in stone or a hard-and-fast rule that says your blog will be more successful if you follow this route. Nor will it likely be less successful by not following this first blog post suggestion. You could just as easily jump right into your first post, covering something specific, and create an "About" page that covers the above information. Further still, some bloggers wish to remain anonymous or vague about their identities, and never go on to create an About page or share information about who they are. This is not representative of most bloggers, however. Having an About page is ideal, because readers will want to know the above information, even if they missed that first blog post where you shared it. Whether you follow the suggested guideline for the first blog post or not, you should include an About page on your blog.

LEGAL CONSIDERATIONS FOR BLOGGERS

Although you are interested in becoming a professional blogger, you are not necessarily coming into this field with a writing background. That's okay! But there are some writing tips that can help you get going. The more you learn about the writing process itself, the easier of a time you may have when it comes to writing your posts.

To get some of the legal matters out of the way first, there are a few issues that you need to be aware of as a professional blogger. These include copyright laws and disclosures. As for copyright laws, you may have learned a bit about this back in high school. Essentially, it is illegal to copy and use someone's work without their consent. Therefore, you cannot simply copy information from someone else and paste it into one of your blog posts and use it as if it were your own.

Having said that, and although it may sound confusing, you can use bits and pieces of it, providing you are giving credit to the source. Additionally, there are some fair-use and copyright-free works that can be used. You just need to be sure that it is copyright free before you proceed to use it. Such work will usually have a stipulation associated with it. For example, if a blogger states that his work is copyright free and that he gives permission to anyone and everyone to use his work free of charge, he may just want to be cited as the author of the work. So as long as you are willing to provide a byline, or a link to the blogger's site (whatever the stipulation may be), then you can use the work free of charge.

When in doubt, always get permission to copy someone else's writing. Some people may grant you permission to use something they have written; you just need to ask them and get their permission in writing. The same goes for photos. Some may be copyrighted, so you need to get permission to use them. However, there are plenty of copyright-free images and free images online. Plus, you can buy some stock images, or stock photo programs, which will give you access to thousands of images that you can use on your site and not have to worry about copyright violations.

There are a few important things that you will want to know when it comes to the area of copyright, including:

- everything you write is automatically copyright protected. As a blogger, you do not need to do anything to further copyright the material. Once you write and post a blog article it is automatically copyright protected in America. The copyright automatically belongs to you, so when you are blogging, don't think you need to do anything else to have your work copyrighted (e.g., register it, make copies of it, etc.).
- many bloggers do take one more step in helping to show that their work is copyright protected. You can do this by putting a copyright notice on your blog, which is usually done in the footer area. To do this, you would simply write something like "© 2013 Jacqueline Bodnar." By placing this notice at the

end of the blog post, or better yet, in the footer of your blog, you are taking one more small measure to protect your work. Registering your blog for copyright protection is generally not necessary.

- everything that is covered under copyright laws includes what people have created, such as written works, pictures, graphics, songs, musical works, and movies.

- all the material that is used on the Internet is copyright protected. Some people mistakenly believe that if it's online that it is somehow not copyright protected. This is simply not true.

- the laws regarding copyrighting allow people "fair use" of other people's work. What this means is that you can use a portion of the person's work. You have probably read some news stories or blog posts by others who have used the fair use laws in order to copy some material from someone else. How this works is that you will see a paragraph, for example, that someone is using as a reference to what their post is about. Let's say you were writing an article about a news story that came out, or about Ernest Hemingway's style of writing. If you had an article you wanted to reference, or a passage you wanted to critique, you could use it wordfor-word up to certain percentage to help demonstrate the point you are making in your post. What's the exact amount that you can copy word-for-word in your article? That's the tough part! There are laws governing what percentage it can be, in regard to the overall length of the project. That could range from 1 percent to 10 percent, or something more. Because it can be a sticky situation, try to minimize what you are copying word-for-word and always be sure to let the reader know where the information came from.

Whether you set the paragraph apart or put it in italics, let the reader know it's not something you wrote. Do let the reader know who wrote the paragraph or sentence.

- generally speaking, government work is copyright free. What that means to people across America is that they can take work that has been produced by the government and copy and use it as they would like to. If there is an article that has been produced by the government, you are free to take the article and copy and paste it into a post on your blog. Their information is copyright free, so you can feel free to use it in most cases. There are a few exceptions, such as if it is work that has been produced by a contractor for the government, but most of their information is copyright free. However, you cannot use their trademarks and logos.

- you do not need to get permission to quote someone, cite their work, or link to their article or site. You also don't need to get permission to use information from a press release. Companies issue press releases hoping that people will snag information from them and use it to give the company free publicity. So feel free to scour press releases for content you think would be a good fit for your blog.

There are a couple of scenarios in copyrighting that you want to be aware of and know how to handle. First off, you may at some point get a message from someone that says you are in copyright violation, that you used or stole the person's work. As you can imagine, this person will be upset. The best way to handle this is professionally. Start by verifying what the person is referring to. A copyright violation occurs when something is taken directly from another person's work without permission. However, you are allowed to cite another person's work or even reproduce a paragraph of it provided you have cited the source. According to the laws regarding this, "fair use" entitles a person to use "limited portions of a work including quotes, for purposes such as commentary, criticism, news reporting, and scholarly reports." (There are no rules stipulating the specific amount of text that can be used, so if you are excerpting from someone else's writing, just try to keep it to a minimum.) If you see that there is no copyright violation, respond in a professional manner to explain that there hasn't been a violation. If you have used a paragraph, and cited who wrote it, let the person know that's part of fair use. If you feel that somehow one slipped past the goalie and there is some sort of copyright violation, promptly remove the work in question from your blog, and write a professional note back to the person explaining that you apologize, that you didn't realize it was in violation, and that it has promptly been removed.

You may also at some time come across your work that has been used without your permission. This has happened to me on numerous occasions. Sometimes it's with your byline, and other times it's not. It's your call if you want to address it. Some people don't mind if their work is used by others, while others may mind a great deal. If you find your work being used without your consent, contact the person doing it, let them know of the violation, and ask that they promptly remove it. Most people are going to comply, because they don't want to cause any problems by keeping it up. You may also want to suggest to them a fee for using the work and see if they are interested in paying it in order to keep the work up on their site. Always be professional when dealing with people, even if you do feel like pulling your hair out due to frustration.

Since you are now savvy on copyright issues, you should be able to avoid violations. But things can happen, or people can get worked up if they see even a paragraph of their work being used in one of your posts. Plus, some people allow guest posts on their blog, and you may not know the origins of that person's work or if there are any violations in it. You can run a quick test on Copyscape.com to see if anything that matches word-for-word exists, but that just means that the search can locate no duplicate copy of it online. It doesn't mean something hasn't been copied out of a book or magazine.

While we are on the topic of offending or upsetting others, it's important to touch on a couple of things. For starters, you should be aware of libel, slander, and defamation. You may have heard these terms before, yet are not completely sure what they mean. As a professional blogger you need to keep them in mind, so that you don't violate them and end up in a lot of hot water.

Libel, slander, and defamation are all acts that can harm a person's reputation or do damage to them or their business. Libel is a written statement about a person or company that is untrue, while slander is spoken statements about a person or company that are not true. The acts of libel and slander both lead to defamation, which harms the reputation of a person or business. The easiest way to avoid these legal problems is to avoid writing things that are untrue. That doesn't mean you can't have an opinion, because you can, but you need to let the reader know you are sharing your thoughts or opinions, so that the statements do not read as though they are true. Defamation occurs when you knew the information was untrue, wrote it, and it led to the person or company's reputation being harmed as a result.

As a writer, you only want to write true information, unless of course you are writing fiction and your readers realize that fact. You are allowed to quote people without their permission, so long as you are quoting them accurately. You should always verify your statistics and details with credible sources before referring to them. For example, if you say that there are 5 million stay-at-home mothers in America, you should verify it, then cite the source (e.g., "According to the U.S. Census Bureau, there are 5 million stay at home mothers in America").

LET YOUR WRITING HAVE A VOICE

One of the greatest pieces of writing advice that I ever received was to write like you talk. At first you may not see the beauty in this, but trust me when I say that reading is much more interesting for the reader when the author writes like they talk. Now you can't do that with every word or sentence, I know, but overall, you should aim to do this. It will bring your writing alive and make it more interesting. Your blog posts are a conversation between you and your readers, so write like you talk, so that your personality comes through and the reader finds it more engaging.

Finding your voice is all about letting your personality come through in your writing. It's what helps to distinguish your work from someone else's. Give your writing a voice. It makes for much more interesting reading, and helps people get to know you and your style. Don't be afraid to let your voice come through in your writing. It's a good thing to give your writing a voice.

ETHICAL BLOGGING

Ethical blogging is largely related to defamation issues. Being a professional means you have not set out to harm any member of the audience. What ethical blogging means in the professional world varies, but would include such issues as having a conflict of interest and not being honest. An example of this would be running a contest on your blog where you say you will randomly draw a winner, and then instead you simply award the prize to your sister or friend. While you may get away with it, it's still an unethical blogging act to engage in. Following blogging ethics at a minimum means never posting things you know are not accurate, not plagiarizing, and letting readers know if what you are reporting is fact (and citing the source of the information) or if it is your opinion. Being an ethical blogger also means correcting errors if you do make them.

IDEAL BLOG POSTS

Know what the perfect blog post is? The one you enjoy reading! Seriously, there is no perfect blog post. There are some guidelines that will help you produce a more user-friendly post, so that it keeps people interested, coming back to read more, and makes it easier to find online. But there is no perfect post. It's largely subjective and based off individual opinions of what each person prefers in an article. So think about it for a moment. You have likely read a lot of blog posts over the last couple of years. What do you like out of a blog post? What is your ideal length and style? Take a moment to grab your blogging notebook and jot down a few things that you like and don't like about blog posts. This will help you identify what your audience may like.

While there is no perfect formula for a winning blog post, there are some rules of thumb you may want to follow and that others have found helpful.

- Blog post length is a big issue. Everyone wants to know what the ideal blog post length is. Well, in all honesty, there isn't a set number. Your ideal length is the number of words it takes for you to convey your information, keeping in mind that your reader has a short attention span. Think about your own reading habits when perusing blog posts. Do you read the entire post, or do you scan it, looking for important tidbits of information? People tend not to spend much time at all on a single web page, so your best bet is to keep it long enough to share the info you want to cover, and short enough that you don't lose their interest. Confusing, right? Well, you have to find what works for you. Typically people would have a blog post that ranges from around 250 words to no more than 1,000 words in length. For my local blog I tend to keep the posts short, sweet, and offer the event information I know the reader will be looking for (e.g., times, dates, addresses). For my other blogs, it varies. If I have a lot to say on a topic I will probably make it around 700 or so words. When ghostwriting for clients, I either go with the length they request, or I suggest a length of around 300 to 400 words.

- If you want to write a particularly long post, say 2,000 words, consider breaking it up into several blog posts, posting them on separate dates, and calling them I, II, and III. That way those interested will continue to read the subsequent posts, rather than people dropping off because they see a super long post and know they don't want to take the time to read it all. If you do break up the posts, always provide the links to the other parts on all posts, so that no matter where someone comes into it they can find the other parts.

- There's no blogosphere police that are going to come and take you away if you don't break up your article in a nice way. However, if you want people to read, and come back to read more, you will try to break up the information so that it is easier for the reader to digest. By this I mean using a nice title and sub-headers, and adding in some bullet points. People are in a hurry, and as such, like to be able to scan the article, read the bullet points, and move on to the next article or site.

- Focus on having a blog title that will engage the reader. It is your title that is usually going to get the person interested in reading the post. Use a strong title that pulls the reader in and makes them want to read more.

- While some may not believe in the hype when it comes to search engine optimization (SEO), it is true that using the right keywords on your blog will help make it show up more in search engine results. SEO will be discussed in depth in chapter seven, when we cover ways to help bring readers to your blog.

- How often you should post is also subjective. Some bloggers post on a weekly basis, or whenever they have a random thought they want to write about, and others post on a daily basis. Some bloggers even post several times per day. There is no right or wrong answer when it comes to frequency. What works for one blog and audience may not work for another. When you start out, plan to put out several blog posts per week, at least until you get some content stocked up on your site. But if the blog you are creating is part of promoting a business (product or service) you may want to put out one post per week, just to keep on your customer's radar screen.

- Blogs are a social media tool, and as such, readers like to have the ability to interact with you, the author. You can do this through allowing comments and replying to some, you can do it via email, or you can even create a page on Facebook. For my local blog I tend to allow comments for a short time, then they automatically close, but I do a lot of interacting with my audience on Facebook. Using Facebook gives me an opportunity to pose questions to them, provide links to additional articles I think they would be interested in, as well as share other items of interest. If you want your readers to interact with you through your blog, then invite them to do so at the end of your posts. Giving them a call to action, such as asking them to leave a comment with their thoughts on the topic, or asking them a question, is an ideal way to get them to comment. People who comment tend to feel like they are a part of the blog and will likely stick around and come back again. It also helps them get to know you better and hopefully the more you get to know your audience the more they suggest your site to others and remain loyal fans.

INCREASING READABILITY

Have you ever thought about the type of blog posts or online articles you like to read? Give it some thought and there's a good chance you may find that you share a lot of reading preferences with others. Keeping these things in mind is not mandatory when writing your blog posts, but doing so will help to make reading easier and more enjoyable for your readers.

- **Headlines.** Aim for having a strong headline for your post. People like to know what it's about and have their interest piqued. If you are going to write about how to end the problem of socks going missing in the dryer, title it something like "5 Tips for Finding Socks in the Dryer."
- **Bullets.** People like to read bulleted lists of information, just as you are reading now. It makes for quick reading that they can scan if they are in a hurry and don't want to read a whole article but want to pick up the important pieces of information.
- **Subheadings**. If your article is going to be on the longer side, break it up with subheadings. This will help keep your reader moving along the page and let them know what to expect in each section. Articles that are long and are not broken up by subheadings and bulleted lists tend to seem overwhelming to some readers and they may just leave your blog with a quick click of the mouse.
- **Bolding.** Having some words be in bold can help the reader to find important information as well. Just by scanning this list of tips you can find the important information, even if you don't go further into reading the explanation of each. While

bolding some words is acceptable, avoid putting words in all caps, as it will be read as shouting.

- **Short sentences.** Hemingway knew what he was doing when he kept sentences short. People like to read short sentences, so if possible, go for shorter sentence lengths.
- **Style.** Unless you are writing for an academic scientific journal, write like you talk for the most part. You want to come across as a real person to your readers and you want them to be comfortable reading what you wrote. If it's stiff and unlike how you would talk in a conversation, it will not be enjoyed by most people. Keeping your sentences conversational, as I have done throughout this book, is a better way to blog. Your personality will come through and your posts will be more enjoyable for the reader.

MORE ON POSTS

As a professional blogger you may want to blog whenever the mood strikes you, or you may want to crank out five posts in one sitting and schedule them to be published later. Blogs allow you to schedule your posts ahead of time. This helps if you want to get a certain amount of work done at once, will be taking a vacation, or would like to work ahead for any other reason. You can set up as many blog posts ahead of time as you want. They won't be published to the masses until the time and date that you scheduled them for.

Having a blog is an effective way of building a platform. A platform is your collective audience, or those who follow what you are doing. There are writers who are looking to be published with publishing houses that will create a blog, establish themselves as an expert on a topic, and then build their audience, or platform. Once they do, they are in a prime position to be able to get book contracts. If your blog has thousands of regular readers, there is a good chance that you can get a book deal to write on that topic, because you have already built a platform.

COMMENTS

I have mentioned comments on blogs, including allowing them, encouraging people to comment, and also closing them. What you do with the commenting option on your blogs is completely up to you, but there are some things you should be aware of. For starters, people like to comment. But it's not always for the reasons you might expect. Many people comment simply to give themselves a link to their own website or blog. I know, shocking, right? But it's true. You may even find yourself doing this as you get going in order to give yourself links to your site (more on this later).

If these commenters are adding to the conversation, and offer a link to their own blog, then it's not an issue. But here's the problem— you will find that many people have nothing to add to the discussion. They simply want to try to plant the free link. Some comments will not even be readable; they are simply generated by a program. Those comments are spam, as they are purely for advertisement purposes and often have nothing to do with your post. For example, you may be blogging about the 2012 Olympic swim team and someone will comment about where you can get the best price on high-end watches. You will spot the spam in seconds once you get started.

Another problem with all the spam and self-promotion is that if your site becomes popular, which you have every intention of it doing, it will take time to monitor all these comments. Most bloggers set their comments to need approval before going live, so that they can do some quality control, only allowing those that make sense to be published. All this monitoring of comments can become time consuming if you start to get a lot of them.

For these reasons, I have learned that allowing open-ended comments to go on forever is not something I want to engage in. I typically set my blog posts to allow for comments for the first two weeks following the post going live, then they automatically close.

I also don't usually encourage or ask people to comment or interact on my blogs. I prefer to do the interaction through my Facebook page, making it quicker to do quality control and less likely someone is out to self-promote and be completely off topic. Taking this route still allows my readers to interact with me, but it saves me the time of monitoring all the comments, and keeps my Facebook page active (which further helps to spread the link to my page and ultimately my blog).

Some popular blogs, such as Leo Babauta's ZenHabits.net, did away with comments a long time ago. His blog, which I regularly read, as do over 250,000 other people, was getting flooded with comments, and it would have taken Leo a lot of time to sift through them, weed out the garbage, and reply. Doing away with the comments on his blog was a smart time-saving move and hasn't hurt his blog's popularity one bit.

THE FIRST MONTH

Everyone starts blogs with high expectations (or at least they should). But the truth is that no matter how great your idea is, or how wonderfully designed your blog may be, there is a good chance that you will need to work hard at building traffic. That's what everyone goes through. Your first month of blogging may leave you feeling lonely. You may long for some comments from readers, just so you know someone is actually reading what you are writing. But stick with it for a while. The first month, or even several months, can be quiet. Building a blog takes time. You need to take the time to build readership and keep people coming back. Don't put a blog up and a week later be bummed out because there's not much traffic. Go into this expecting that your first month, and for a while thereafter, is going to be quiet and likely low in traffic. But the longer you stick with it, the more posts you will publish and the more readers you will gain.

Blogging is certainly not a get-rich-quick type of scam. You can absolutely make money, and even make a living, being a professional blogger. But whether you are running your own blogs, blogging for others, or doing a combination of both, you will have to be realistic and give it some time. You need to build an audience. There isn't an audience sitting there twiddling their thumbs just waiting for you to publish your first post. In order to gain their readership you will need to find them, draw them in, retain them, and keep on keeping on!

MAINTAINING YOUR BLOG

Once you have your blog, or blogs, up and running, you need to maintain them. When people land on your blog and they find that it hasn't been updated in weeks, months, or in some cases years, it's a turn off. If you have an interest in being a successful blogger you will need to maintain your blogs. Here are a few things you will want to do in order to maintain your blog.

- Look at it regularly. It seems simple enough, yet there are some people who may not even think to look at their own blog. As you are looking at it, notice if everything is working properly.
- Keep publishing content. Maybe you start out of the gate posting on a daily basis, and then you start to slow down and run out of ideas to blog about. You still need to keep publishing fresh content. Pace yourself, and find new ideas or expand upon ones you have already blogged about, but keep publishing new content.
- Continue publishing during down times. If you usually publish every other day, or every week, and you will be going on vacation for a couple of weeks, you can still

publish a post during that time. Write the posts ahead of time and schedule them to run on the days when you would normally post.

- Maintaining your blog, as well as your enthusiasm for blogging, is important to being a professional blogger. An ignored or neglected blog cannot bring you advertisers, and may not bring you additional paid blogging opportunities.

Chapter Six
Beyond Penning Posts

*"Happiness lies in the joy of achievement and the thrill
of creative effort."*
—Franklin D. Roosevelt

Blogging can be a lot of fun. But if you are not someone who enjoys writing, you may find that it's more like work than it is fun or interesting. There are some things you can do to enhance your blogging effort and to help keep it a little more interesting, for both you and your audience.

As you are in the process of building your blog, and as you go along maintaining it, you will likely think of some new features you would like to add. Don't be afraid to give it a shot and see if it works. If it does, great! If it doesn't, you have not lost anything but the time you put in to try it.

VLOGGING
Have you ever landed on a blog that is a video to watch, rather than an article to read? That's referred to as a "vlog," short for a video blog. Vlogs are a popular route for those who want to have a blog but do not want to write the posts. See, even if you are not

a writer, or don't want to become one, you can still have a type of blog. A vlog makes it easy for anyone with a video camera to get started.

Just about everyone today has some sort of video recording capabilities available. Whether on your cell phone, handheld recorder, or on your webcam (Internet camera), you can easily record videos, and then post them to your vlog when you are ready. The options with vlogging are plentiful. You can vlog with you speaking, so that you are looking into the camera and sharing what you would otherwise be putting into an article, or you can record other things to share with your audience.

Let's say you want to have a vlog that covers traveling in the area where you live. You could take video footage of all kinds of things that tourists would be interested in, and then create individual vlog posts featuring each video. You could also have one with a local news focus. What your theme is does not really matter so much (unless it's pornographic in nature, of course). You can create a recorded vlog post covering just about anything. If you like cooking and want to have a blog focused on how to make the best cupcakes in the world, you will want to record yourself making some cupcakes. People are visual and like to see things happening.

Vlogging is a great way to connect with your audience, especially if you will be seen and heard on the recording. It gives your personality and voice a chance to be heard and resonate with the audience. It is possible to have solely a vlog, rather than a blog, and be every bit as successful. So if you don't like writing all those posts, and prefer using your video camera, consider all of the vlogging opportunities that exist.

If you are going to have a vlog, rather than a blog, you will also have a learning curve, just like with getting started in blogging. Do your homework to learn all you can about the process, but realize you will get better with practice. There are issues to keep in mind when it comes to recording your videos, especially if you will be featured talking in them, including:

- editing. You will want to learn how to edit so that you can remove mistakes or cut out parts that are unnecessary.
- angles and lighting. It may seem like this is a no-brainer, but once you start recording you may find that you need to learn more about these things.
- video length. You will need to determine what the ideal length for conveying your information is and that your audience is patient enough to watch. Most people will watch a video that is a minute or two, for example, but make it fifteen minutes long and you will most likely lose your viewers after a few minutes at the most (unless it's really good!). Watch some other vlogs and see what catches your attention and how long you can watch before you tend to get bored and want to click away.
- background images. If you will be talking on video you will want to be aware of what is behind you. Some things will come across more flattering on camera than others.
- outlining what you will be discussing. Just turn the camera on and start talking and you may stumble over what it was you wanted to bring up in the first place. It's always a good idea to outline, or jot down a list of things that you plan to talk about.
- music. This is especially helpful if you have made videos that have an opening introduction. There are other times you may want to add in music as well, which can either be your own, or you can purchase stock music to add to videos. Avoid using

a copyrighted piece of music without permission or without purchasing the rights to use it first.

- incorporating visuals. These may be charts, pictures, or graphic images that will enhance what is being talked about. For example, if you are creating a cooking video, you may want to add a screen shot of the recipe.

These are all somewhat advanced vlogging issues, but information on them is widely available, and you will learn many of them through trial and error as you go along. There is a lot to learn in vlogging, just like with blogging.

Even if you decide to do a vlog, it's still a good idea to have at least a short paragraph with each one. The paragraph can be used to let the audience know what to expect from the video, but it can also help pull in traffic by using the right SEO keywords. Also, even if you don't plan to have a vlog, you can add more interest to your blog by posting some occasional videos. They will help to enhance your audience's experience by adding some variety to your site.

Similar to a vlog, some people have photo blogs. These are blogs that are made up of mainly images, but usually have some type of heading or short paragraph to accompany each one. This may be a route that a photographer would take.

CONTESTS AND GIVEAWAYS

Blogs are popular for having contests and giveaways, which is great for getting people's interest. They also give something back to your audience, even if it is only one winner for each contest. At least the chance to win something is there, which people tend to like. Having contests and giveaways on your blog is just one more way to add another layer of interest and stickiness, which means it helps to keep people coming back to see what you will be giving away next.

If you have your own product or service that you are promoting on your blog, then you may want to give away your own products and services as the prize. For example, if you have published a book or you run a local cleaning service, you could offer a monthly contest to give away a free book or free cleaning service. If you do not have a product or service of your own to give away, don't worry, there are plenty of products you can get from others to give away.

Both local and national companies are usually willing to give away a product or service on your site. All you need to do is contact them and see if they would like to team up to give away something on your blog. Doing this through email will take you about a minute. Copy and paste the email to repeat and send to other companies. You could find one product to give away, or you may come back with multiple ones and you can have a "12 days of giving" contest on your blog.

In setting up the contests and giveaways, you will want to keep the following things in mind.

- **Ethics.** If someone is giving you a prize to give away, don't try to keep it for yourself, or give it away to your daughter or best friend. Be fair in running your contest by making sure the person is randomly drawn (or however you state the winner will be chosen), and don't try to rig it so that your buddy wins.

- **Promoting.** Once you have your prizes to give away, write up an intriguing post to let people know of the contest. Explain clearly what the prizes to be awarded are, how people can enter, when the contest will end, when the winner will be announced, and any other disclaimers that are necessary. Spell out as much detail as you can, so that you don't leave yourself open for questions later on. If there is a value, restrictions, or other details that readers will want to know about, be sure to include it. You don't want someone winning a prize and then coming back to say that they thought they were getting something else. Make your contest as clear and foolproof as possible. If you use Facebook or Twitter, be sure to give the contest plugs throughout its duration to increase exposure.

- **Prizes.** Try to either get the prizes in your hand, and you give them away (or send a gift card), or get it in writing that the sponsoring company will be supplying the prize to the winner. Even a saved email communication from the company, where they have agreed to the contest and giving away a prize, will serve as evidence if they fail to live up to their end of the bargain.

- **Entries.** You will need to determine how you want people to enter the contest. There are many ways you can do it and you can use your imagination to come up with more creative ideas. Typically, bloggers have people enter by leaving a comment on the blog, providing a link to the blog somewhere, or voting on something. You can use any method that you believe you can logistically get to work for you, but be sure to clearly state what you expect entrants to do in order to be qualified for the contest.

- **Rules.** As mentioned above, be sure to write up a paragraph that spells out the rules of the contest. Don't leave anything open to personal interpretation. Always be clear and precise. The clearer you are with your rules up front, the fewer possible problems could arise later on.

- **Winners.** Whether you have one winner or several, you need a fair way to choose them. This can be a tough task. Work it out ahead of time. Decide if the winner is chosen by public voting, randomly drawn, or whatever you believe will work for the type of contest you are having. Once you have the names of the winners, write a blog post to announce them, and post that announcement on your Facebook or Twitter page. Email the winners to inform them they have won and let them know how they will get their prize (they need to contact a company to set something up, or it will come in the mail, etc.). Save copies of these emails in a contest folder until all the prizes have been received.

On my local blog I have had several contests. The only thing that I tend to get out of them is the satisfaction of giving something back to my readers, which tends to build loyalty and increase word-of-mouth advertising. Securing prizes to give away is fairly easy. All I have to do is ask a local company and they are usually willing to do it in exchange for the free publicity. You could also charge a fee for doing this, especially if you were doing it with a national company, and if you could give them a lot of advertisement as a result.

My blog has featured contests giving away a massage, surf camp, gymnastics lessons, and other things. Personally, when it comes to prizes, I prefer to have the company who is giving the prize send it directly to the winner. I prefer to take this route mainly because it saves me time. By having the company who's giving the prize away ship it directly, or arrange it with the person, I don't have to get involved. If I had to ship the prizes it would cost me the time of having to prepare the item, take it to the post office, and try to ensure the winner received it. I can leave all that behind by simply having it sent directly to the winner.

Usually the longest that I run contests is around two weeks. I have found that if I do it longer most people tend to lose interest after a while, and if I do it for a much shorter time period I don't feel like the advertiser is getting enough exposure or that it gives all of my audience a chance to learn of the contest and enter. Once the contest is over, I tend to go back into that blog post and in italics I post a paragraph at the top of the page stating the contest is over and offering the name of the winner. I do this so that the blog post can stay up on my blog, but it doesn't cause any confusion. I don't want anyone finding it later on and trying to enter even though it's long been over.

Most blog contests seem to go just fine. I haven't heard or read of a lot of problems that have resulted from them. But from time to time some things can happen, and something may fall through. I ran one contest where the person was having a hard time claiming the prize from the company that was supposed to be supplying it. Even after speaking with the company about it I didn't feel comfortable that they were going to come through. In that event, all you can do is offer an apology, and if you have the ability to, offer a replacement prize.

When it comes to choosing the contest or giveaway winners on my blog, I try to keep it simple. When I created the first one I researched various ways to have people enter, and to pull winners. I like to keep it simple so that it doesn't take a lot of time, because that's time that I could be doing something else, like writing. I typically have people enter the contest by leaving a comment on the blog post. I have them answer a question. Since it is a local blog, I try to get them to answer a question that will add some additional keywords to my blog. For example, I might ask them where their favorite park in the community is, or something that is related to the theme of the contest. The comments are all "numbered" in the order they are received. Then when I need to pull the winner, I use Random.org, which is a site where you plug in the two numbers consisting of your beginning (1) and ending (number of entrants you received). So if I had 30 people enter the contest, I would enter that I need a random number between 1 and 30. Hit the button, and within seconds you have your winner. The site randomly offers you a number. Then just go back and look at your entrants to find who had that particular number. It's a fair, unbiased method for pulling the winner, and it takes seconds.

Running contests and giveaways is not something you have to do with your blog. But it can be a good way to build a buzz, get new people interested, and add a little fun to your blog. You can always try having one and see how it goes, then determine if you want to have more. Once you have done the first one they are often easier, because you can copy your rules and use them again in the new contest. All you will need to do is plug in the info on the new one, including what's being given away, and the dates the contest runs.

FUN WITH WIDGETS

"Widgets" may seem like an odd name for these handy little applications you can add to your blog, but they can be great. They are easy to use, often free, will enhance your reader's experience, and can even increase the number of pages people view.

One of the widgets that I use on my blogs is LinkWithin. It's a free application that takes seconds to set up and it offers up thumbnail pictures to your readers of additional blog posts they may be interested in reading. You may have seen these before and didn't realize that's what it was. At the bottom of some blog posts you will see a phrase like, "You might also like:" and then it offers up several thumbnail pictures and blog post titles. That's a widget, and it automatically generates those suggestions to your reader. It helps to keep people reading additional posts on your site.

There are a lot of widgets available and most of them fit nicely into the margins of your blog. You can do a quick Google search for "blog widgets" to see some of the latest options that are available to you. There are widgets that will show how many people are reading the blog, where they are from, page ranking information, visitor number information, horoscopes, polls, maps, and more. There is a good chance that there are a couple of widgets you may want to add to your blog.

GUEST BLOGGING

The idea of guest blogging can go two ways. First off, you can write guest posts for other people's blogs in exchange for getting a link back to your own blog. This can be a viable way of promoting your own blog and many people do engage in it. You would simply find blogs that cover themes complementary to yours, contact the blogger, and offer to write a guest post in exchange for the link back to your own. If they are interested in this, they will want it to fit the theme of their blog and will usually want it to be a unique post, meaning that it is not running elsewhere already.

On the other end, you will likely have a lot of people approach you about guest blogging. It's totally up to you whether or not you want to accept guest posts. If you do, be sure to put a byline on them and let your readers know they are reading a guest post, so they don't assume it is one by you. Other things to keep in mind are that you want the post to fit into your blog theme, and that the post is not plagiarized. Run a quick Copyscape.com search in order to verify that the information is not copied from somewhere online.

Most likely, a lot of bloggers will offer you guest posts. This is because, like the ones that you would offer, they are seeking self-promotion. It's okay to turn some or all of them down. Don't feel obligated to take guest posts from people. Remember that it's your blog and you are responsible for retaining your audience and for maintaining quality control. If you are not interested in any guest blog posts, you may want to make that disclaimer on your site. If you do accept them, state that you will review them and are selective in only choosing ones that closely match your blog theme. If you want to accept a lot of guest blog posts, and some people do, you may want to create a whole page explaining the guidelines of what you are looking for, such as unique content, theme, word count preference, and how you prefer the article be sent in to you. Depending on your blog, it may not make sense to include some guest posts.

Having guest bloggers on your site is just an option; you don't have to offer it. Some people like to offer guest posts because it gives them more content without more work. Others prefer not to—their blog is always them and their own voice. There is no right or wrong on this issue. It is a matter of personal preference and what you feel will be the best move for your blog. I have had a couple of guest posts in the past, but I prefer not to have them, because I feel that I don't get much out of it. To me it seems that the one submitting the guest post is the one that stands to gain from it the most. But some people find it useful and like to offer the additional content on their site. In fact, some blogs are built around having numerous writers, but this is a different issue and can be quite successful.

Another option is to charge for the guest post placement, which would be like paid editorials or advertorials in a magazine. If you have a company that would like a post about them on your blog, or who wants to submit a post to promote their company, you can charge for this service. This is known as "pay per post" and is used by many bloggers. It's really just another form of advertising. Be sure to keep blogging disclosure laws in mind, which will be covered in chapter nine.

AUDIO PODCASTING

Audio podcast episodes are another option for enhancing your blog. These are downloadable audio files that people can listen to. They

81

can download them on their computer, phone, or even their iPod. This gives them the opportunity to listen to you even while they are not at their computer. This is a popular format that some people use when they want to focus on one issue and talk about it for a longer period of time. Podcasts are often thirty to sixty minutes in length and listeners can hit pause when they need to. They can even listen to them while they are taking a walk or working.

If you decide to create podcasts, be sure to do your homework first to get the inside scoop on how to pull it off professionally. Visit the iTunes website and read their guide to making podcasts. You will want to consider such issues as editing, background noise, your topic, length, and writing an outline or notes about what you will talk about in your podcast, prior to getting started. If podcasts interest you, first listen to some others in order to see what you like and don't like. Popular podcasts include the *Stanford Entrepreneurial Thought Leaders Series*, *Intelligence Squared*, *Zig Ziglar*, and *TEDTalks*. Take notes, and use them to formulate the best approach for your own podcasts. When posting your podcasts, write a paragraph to let the audience know what to expect when listening to each segment.

PICKING PHOTOS

One thing that can enhance a blog post is to have at least one picture. Not everyone includes them, but if they can add to the post, then it's a nice touch. The pictures you take yourself are the best ones. This is especially true if your posts offer reviews of products, traveling, or other tangible items. Take some good pictures and post them with your blog post.

If you would like to use generic stock images, you can find plenty of royalty-free ones online, or you can purchase them inexpensively through online services and programs. Check around and compare pricing. Some sites charge more than others, and there are even free clip art and stock photography options available.

Some people may have questions about whether or not they can personally take a picture of something and then put it on their blog. If you personally take pictures of something, you do not need to get permission to use them on your blog. As a blogger you are acting as a journalist and you are covered under freedom of the press laws. You can legally post any pictures or videos on your blog that you have taken, or that one of your colleagues has taken (as opposed to needing permission if you want to use a photographer's work on your site, for example). So don't be afraid to post your photos and videos on your blog.

Having said that, there is one thing you do have to be cautious about, and that is recording someone without their knowledge of it. That is not legal and can get you into a lot of hot water. For example, don't call someone up on the phone with a hidden voice recorder, ask them some burning questions, and then put the recording on your blog. If you didn't disclose to the person that they were being recorded it has been conducted illegally. Any time you are going to record someone's voice, such as in an interview, always disclose on the tape (so that it is also recorded) that you are going to tape the conversation.

One thing you don't want to do is to take pictures and then alter them to change their integrity (unless your site is a parody and people realize that is the goal). Editing the lighting or cropping is one thing, but using a program like Photoshop to make a person look fatter, thinner, appear with someone, or do anything else to change the integrity of the photo or alter what the image originally was would not be ethical and could lead to problems. Short of cleaning up the picture for online use, avoid doing anything to it that would change what was really going on when you snapped the photo.

BEYOND BASICS

As you can see, there are a lot of additional things you can do beyond penning posts on your blog. You may want to include some or all of these, or you may want to skip them altogether. The choice, like your blog, is all yours to make. Use what you think will enhance your blog, and skip what you think won't. Try a few things and see what the outcome is and if you want to continue or do it again. There's no harm in trying one of these options, or others, to test it out and see how it goes. You are not boxed into sticking with anything you try. The options and flexibility are always there for you to make changes and take things in a new direction.

Chapter Seven
Promoting and Getting Noticed

"Before everything else, getting ready is the secret of success."
—Henry Ford

The idea that if you build it, they will come may sound nice in theory, but it doesn't exactly work like that in the business world. Sure, some things may sell like hotcakes simply because you opened the doors on the business, but the majority of successful businesses need to work at it in order to become successful.

If you want to succeed as a professional blogger, you must take on a business mentality. Your blogging is your business, whether you are doing it for your own blogs, or are being paid to do it for other blogs. Professional bloggers are in the business of selling blogging skills. What does this mean for you on a day-to-day basis? A lot!

As a professional blogger you will have to avoid, as much as possible, writing blog posts for free or for low wages that won't pay your bills at the end of the day or month. When people learn that you have become a professional blogger you will begin to get friends, family members, charities, and even businesses you don't know approaching you to see if you will write them some blog posts. They may even want you to manage their blogs. It's only a problem if they want you to do it for free or for wages so low you can't pay your bills, or that you spend so much time taking on their low-paying work that you don't have time to focus on higher-paying blogging positions.

Whether or not to write for free is an age-old debate in the writer's world. On the one hand people argue that it can give you exposure and help get your name out there. On the other hand, which is the one that I tend to agree with, it cheapens the profession and keeps you making low wages. Remember what I said about thinking like a business. Do businesses give away free services to those who walk through their door asking for it? Perhaps on a limited basis, but it has to be a very limited basis if they want to survive and thrive. Whether or not you agree to blog for free, or low wages, is completely up to you. That's not to say that there are never acceptable times to write something for free, not at all. But it does mean that if you want to make a living as a professional blogger you will have to be selective, and limiting, in the amount of work you are willing to do for free. Weigh the advantages to ensure that you are getting enough out of it. But let it be known that the more bloggers are willing to blog for free, or for a couple of dollars per post, the less people will be willing to pay decent wages to professional bloggers.

TRAFFIC IS KEY

In thinking of your blogging as a business, which it is if you are making it more than a hobby, there is one major thing you need to be successful. That one major thing is traffic to your blog. Getting traffic to your blog is going to be one of the biggest challenges you face, but it is certainly one that you can take on and beat. For starters, you can submit your blog to search engines. If you visit the search engines you will typically see a link somewhere near the bottom of the page, usually at the bottom, for submitting your blog URL. Just fill in the page and submit it. However, even if you don't take the time to do this your blog is going to end up showing up in search engines. Yet taking the time to submit may get it picked up quicker.

There are a variety of ways that you can get traffic to your blog. In this chapter we will explore some of the more popular routes that bloggers take in order to do just that. Why is it so important to have traffic to your blog? Because those are the people who are going to buy whatever it is that you are selling, regardless of whether it is a product, service, or an idea. You need people reading your blog on a regular basis in order to make all your efforts worthwhile (unless you are doing all this for a hobby, rather than to be a professional blogger, of course). Moreover, it's important to have a lot of traffic to your website because the more traffic you have, the more valuable your advertising space will be to those looking to reach your readers. Having a popular blog that gets a lot of traffic will also help you in ways that you may not see right away, earning you book and business deals, guest speaker invitations, free products to review, and more.

FINDING YOUR AUDIENCE

The people you want to reach are your audience. As you are blogging, think of yourself as standing on a stage in front of them in an auditorium. Write your posts to that group of people. But first, try to define who those people are. The more you know about your potential audience, the more you will know where and how to reach them. If you know the things that your audience likes to read, where they go, and what they do for fun, you will be able to use that information to reach and pull them into your blogging world.

Once you find your audience you want to focus on finding more people, of course, but you also want to keep your audience. Having your audience at your site will only make you successful if you keep them. Keeping them shouldn't be difficult if you are still giving them what they came to the blog for. If they visit your site for insightful tips on having backyard bird feeders, then as long as you keep providing content that is somehow related to that, even if you broaden your scope a little more, they should stay there. This is providing that you don't do something to offend them. You will always lose a few people here and there, because you can't please everyone no matter how hard you try, and some people may decide that the topic isn't for them. But you want to focus on keeping the majority of your audience constant, as well as continuing to grow your audience.

SUBSCRIBING

Finding multiple ways for your audience to keep in contact and keep getting your blog posts is crucial. You can do this in a variety of ways, choosing one or all of them, depending on your preferences. Some readers prefer to get their blog posts through Feedburner, which is a management tool. Others may prefer to get an email each time you publish new blog posts. You can also use other social media tools to keep in touch with your audience and send them links to your new posts.

My blogs typically have a variety of ways that people can continue to keep up on the information I'm publishing. I have the option to sign up for email subscriptions or Feedburner, which is a blog post management tool that helps share and track all blog post feeds, and I also use Facebook and Twitter. So each time I publish a new blog post it is automatically sent out (once per day) to my email subscribers and is added to the feed that is provided to those using Feedburner. It is also automatically sent to those following my blog on Twitter. The only one that I manually add is on Facebook. You could set it up to automatically post there, but I like to interact with my followers there.

Another option is to use the RSS, which stands for Really Simple Syndication, to allow people to easily syndicate your content. RSS is helpful to readers of your blog because when they subscribe all your new blog posts will arrive in their readers. The reader gives the subscriber the ability to see all new posts and articles from their favorite sites all in one place, rather than having to visit multiple sites or read numerous emails to get all the new articles. As a blogger, RSS can be a helpful tool in getting your blog posts shared and growing your audience. RSS is not only a popular way for people to help promote their site, but it is also free. So you really don't have anything to lose by adding this feature to your blog. It may help you get more traffic with just the effort of setting the syndication tool up on your blog.

Re-blogging is another option that allows people to re-blog your content on their own blog. Some people find this to be a helpful tool in promoting their blogs, while others feel it is merely giving people content for free. There are quite a few options when it comes to all these tools and applications that can be added to your blog. Your best bet is to research them to see if they sound like something you would like to utilize. Keep in mind that you are not bound to keep them if they don't work out. You can always give it a try to see how you like it, and do away with it if you find it doesn't suit your needs or purpose.

As a blogger there are a variety of ways that you can interact with your audience. When you interact with them it gets them more interested in your blog, and it will end up boosting your work, whether in page views, items sold, or by referrals. When you build a relationship with those that follow your blog, they will end up feeling more loyal to you and will also often help build your audience.

If you are using Facebook you can easily interact with your audience there. I tend to post questions and try to interact with my blog audience frequently. I will even post news articles related to my topic, if I think it is something that they would be interested in. Many people are also opting to use Pinterest, an online pinboard where users can post images and links to things they like, in an effort to take a more visual route to interact with their audience.

As previously mentioned, commenting is another way to interact with your audience. Many bloggers keep the comments option open on their blog posts, allowing their readers to provide instant feedback to the post. It gives your readers an opportunity to interact and respond to each other, and gives you the ability to respond to them. Essentially, a conversation can take place in the comments section if you choose to allow it. Whether or not you open comments up to your readers is up to you and based on your preference. As described earlier, allowing comments on your blog has both pros and cons. The more popular your blog, the more time you will find yourself policing the comments and trying to keep out those that are off topic, are pure spam, or contain language that could offend some of your readers.

When I first started my blogs in 2009 I allowed comments for an unlimited amount of time. But I found after a while that I would have to spend time going through them to delete all the spam and it got old quickly. Even those that seemed like they were legitimate comments usually came with some sort of link, making me think it was more about advertising their site, rather than interacting on my blog. Following this experience, I changed the settings on my blog to allow comments for only a two-week period. For me, this is a happy medium, allowing people to comment if they would like to, but closing it for all the spammers who tend to find the posts later on.

It's also a good idea to list an email address on your blog, so that people have a way to contact you. Not only is this good for your followers, but it also gives potential advertisers and sponsors a way to contact you as well. To help avoid additional spam in the email box you may want to type out the address in such a way that it is not picked up by bots (web robots). Such software scours the Internet snagging email addresses and then adding them to mailing lists so that the person gets oodles of messages and wonders how all these places got their email address. On your contact page, or contact link, you can write your address out to help avoid this (ContactMe @ MyBlog Dot com). Just write a quick message explaining that people need to remove the spaces and use the "." rather than "dot." Most people are familiar with seeing this and realize it is to keep you from getting spammed like there's no tomorrow. Also, you may want to set up a separate email address for all this communication, rather than putting your personal one online for the world to see, have, and possibly even sell to marketers.

On your contact page you may also want to make a little disclaimer about how you get a lot of mail and it may take some time to respond. That way people will not be looking for a quick response, because the truth is that the more popular your blog is the longer it probably will take you to respond to people. There's a good chance that you will get a lot of email communication once your blog becomes popular. Some of it may be of interest to you, some could lead to money and review products, and a lot of it may be pure garbage that you want to hit the delete key on.

USING SEO TO BUILD TRAFFIC

If you haven't yet heard of SEO, which stands for "search engine optimization," then you are about to enter its realm and get real cozy. SEO is using keywords in your blog posts and blog, rather than using paid advertising, in an effort to draw in traffic to your blog. There are some people who are not fans of or believers in SEO and may even speak out against it. But most bloggers do incorporate some SEO into their blogging, or at a minimum have it in the back of their mind as they add in a few specific words here and there.

SEO is about the algorithms that are used that can bring up your blog in search engine results. Here are a couple of examples of blog title headers to give you an idea of what SEO is and how it works.

> *We provide the best plumbing services around. Call us!*
> *Las Vegas plumbing services, serving the entire valley. Call*
> *702-Get-Nope*

In the first example it will be difficult for that site to show up in someone's search engine results, because there's nothing real specific there. If someone is in Las Vegas, or in Des Moines, and they need a plumber, they are not likely to go to a search engine and simply type in "plumbing services." That would yield millions of results that may not be anywhere close to where they are, depending on their search factors. However, in the second one the company is more likely to have a chance of showing up when someone goes to the search engine and types in "Las Vegas plumbing."

SEO helps the reader, or searcher, find your site, and it helps the search engines to know what your site is about, so they can pull up relevant information to provide people when they do their searches. It's important to use some keywords in your posts and on your site, even if you don't put a lot of emphasis on using SEO. At a bare minimum you should take it into account when you set up your blogs, so that there are keywords in your blog title bar, as well as in your blog titles and subheadings.

On your own personal blogs you can choose to use as much, or as little, SEO as you would like. But if you are going to be offering professional blogging to paid clients, there is a good chance they will not only be familiar with it, but will request it. So you will need to familiarize yourself with it. Knowing how to write SEO blog posts is important in making a living as a professional blogger, especially if you plan to write posts for paying clients.

Here some tips to keep in mind when using SEO in your blog post writing.

- You still want your blog posts to sound as natural as possible for the reader. So even though you may be adding in some keywords to help with search engine results, you need to make sure the information reads correctly, and naturally, to the reader.

- To determine your SEO keywords, think like your audience. If someone were to want your information, or blog, what words would they type into the search engine in order to find it? Use some of those. You need to think like your audience in order to determine what words will be meaningful to them and used by them when they go looking for information.

- You can use online keyword generators, such as the Google AdWords Tool, in order to get keyword ideas. Just go to Google and type in "AdWords Tool" and it will come up. Start out by typing in your topic and see what results it brings up. The tool will generate a long list of possible related keywords and phrases. It will also give you information about how many Google domestic and global searches there are each month for each keyword. Using this will not only help you generate ideas for possible keywords to use, but it will let you know if people are searching for the ones you are using.

- Keyword density is another issue that will come up when it comes to writing SEO blog posts. This refers to how often the keyword is used throughout the post. The preference on this varies, with many people preferring to have the keywords make up around 1 to 3 percent of your total word count. However, I have been paid many times to write SEO blog posts for clients who required a 5 percent keyword density. The keyword density is determined by the percentage of copy containing a given keyword or keyword phrase. For example, if you are writing an article for someone and your keyword is "magnetic name badges," you will want to use that string of words as often as necessary to reach the percentage that your client has indicated (usually ranging from 1–5 percent). This means that if you are writing a four hundred-word article, you want that keyword or keyword phrase to appear twenty times in order to reach a 5 percent density. You do not have to count each of these instances yourself; there are live keyword analysis tools available for free online. Simply copy and paste your article into the online form, type in your keyword, and it will tell you the keyword density. You can then adjust it accordingly to meet your needs or those of your client.

Your best bet is to find what you are comfortable with for your own blog, and do the keyword density your clients request if you are being paid to write blog posts for others. Not everyone considers keyword density when writing their posts. If you do, there are plenty of keyword density tools online that you can use for free. Just pull one up, copy in your article, type in your keywords, and it will give you the keyword density percentage. You can make changes right on the page to get it to the percentage that you prefer. If you are writing posts for your own blog you will not have to be as concerned with keyword density. In my experience, this has mainly been an issue when doing paid blogging work for others.

- Tagging and categories on your blog help your readers to locate information, will organize your blog posts, and can also be helpful in your blog being picked up by search engines. Think of categories as files. When you write blog posts you will chose a file, or category, to place it in. Try to avoid going overboard with the number of categories you have. If you have too many it just makes for a long list that people are not likely sift through. It's also important to tag your blog posts, which is adding an appropriate keyword about what the post is about. Try to limit the number of tagging keywords you are using, making sure to be consistent in using the same words for like posts.

- Using link exchanges and blogrolls can be an effective way to increase traffic on your site. These are links to other blogs that you provide on your own blog. In theory, the other bloggers will reciprocate and also provide their readers with a link to your blog. Many people are fans of using a link exchange or blogroll on their site. If you do go this route, try to find other blogs that cover a similar topic or complementary one, so the audience will likely have some interest in your blog. Also, it helps if you are able to exchange links with a blog that gets a fairly good amount of traffic to begin with. If their blog doesn't get much traffic, the link exchange is not likely to bring you many additional readers.

- For around $20 you can have some professional business cards made up online. These can be small, effective tools in helping to get information out about your own blogs, as well as the fact that you are a blogger for hire. Hand them out when networking, if you are mailing an invoice for the first time, and use them any other time you think it makes sense to do so. They are an inexpensive marketing tool that can bring your blog traffic, and can lead to additional blog writing projects.

ADDITIONAL PROMOTION

When it comes to the many ways that you can promote your blog, you are really only limited by your own imagination. The opportunities are there, you just need to determine which ones make sense for you, and then incorporate them into your plan. What works for one blogger may not produce such great results for another. Additional promotional opportunities range from advertising and sponsorships to teaching classes and offering talks at conferences.

There are promotional opportunities within your own community, if you have a local blog, as well as on a national scale, if your target audience is a national one. To give you an example of the range of opportunities that exist, to help promote my local blog, I became a sponsor in a local 5K race that took place. I was able to have a professional postcard promoting my local blog put into the goodie bag of each of the participating runners. That morning a couple of hundred people got a postcard, learning more about my blog. This was a low-cost method of reaching people in the community, costing me only around $50 total for the exposure. Plus, it gave me a chance to offer support to a community event.

Another way you can increase traffic to your site is to get some free publicity. Write and issue a press release whenever you have something to announce, and send it out to the appropriate media outlets. Be sure to write a professional press release or it will be deleted faster than you can imagine. If you are not experienced in writing press releases, take the time to do some online research and learn how to write a professional one. Using a press release can be especially helpful in getting noticed if you have a local blog. You can write a press release announcing news and submit it to local media outlets.

Whether you have a local, national, or global-appealing blog you can use public relations to gain some free exposure. It's especially helpful if you can get quoted in articles, so make a point to send your press releases to reporters who cover your area of blogging interest.

There are also blogger conferences that take place throughout the year. Many bloggers find the investment in them to be worthwhile. At conferences you will have the opportunity to learn, network, and even possibly get a chance to share what you know to help build your own name. Depending on what you blog about, there are blogger conferences for everyone, ranging from general ones to those who cover niches such as mommy and vegan blogging. It's also a good idea to attend conferences that are not focused on bloggers, but may be a gold mine for finding people who are interested in your blog topic or who would be interested in hiring a blogger. Be sure to attend such conferences with a stack of business cards in hand, and be ready to give people your elevator speech on what your blogging skills can do for their business. Gather business cards there as well, so that you can follow up with contacting the people you met and offer your blogging services.

As already discussed, additional social media outlets can be effective in helping to promote your site. Sites such as Twitter, Facebook, YouTube, and Pinterest, among others, can be great places for gaining new traffic to your blog. If you don't want to take the time to set up accounts on all of them, choose one to start with and go from there to see if you want to add another later on.

One of the most effective ways to get traffic to your blog is through word-of-mouth referrals. If people like your blog they are bound to tell others about it. One of my favorite blogs for years has been the ZenHabits.net blog, which I wrote about earlier. I can't tell you how many people I have personally referred to that blog. Over the years that I have been reading it, I have recommended it to many people and continue to do so periodically. When we find things that we like, or that we feel can be beneficial or interesting to others, we tend to want to share it, whether it's a silly dog picture online that has a funny caption, or it's a blog that you have taken a liking to. So get your readers to like your blog, and they will help to do some of the promoting for you.

Whether you have bumper stickers made up of your blog address and hand them out to everyone at a festival, or you teach a blogging class at your local community center, there are many ways to promote your blog. All you need to do is find the ones that appeal to you, and then make it happen.

KEEPING READERS

If you review the Alexa stats from many blogs you will see that people don't usually stay long on any particular site. Some readers may spend a mere thirty to sixty seconds at a site. In your quest to keep people on the site longer and reading more pages, which will help increase your page views, you can do a number of things. For starters, if you are writing about something in a blog post that you can link to another post you have written it can help get them to click on the other one and read it as well. Including internal links to other posts within your blog post is helpful in increasing traffic and keeping your audience reading longer. If you have written about the topic in a similar post, highlight it with a link in the current one you are writing.

Make good use of your category sections as well. You don't want to have a huge list of them, as it won't be as effective, but if you can narrow it down to the most important ones, your readers will be more inclined to click on them to scroll through the category. Another way that some bloggers increase page views is to use excerpts, rather than full blog posts on particular pages. This would mean that instead of someone visiting your blog home page and seeing full blog posts, they would see excerpts, or short snippets, of the full blog post. In order to read the full blog post they would need to click on the link and go to that blog post page. Some people don't care for using excerpts, but if readers like your content it is unlikely that they will leave your site simply because they have to click a link to read the full story.

Whether you do it once a year or every few months, you can create a blog post that contains your most popular posts. That will give people a list of links to ten to twenty blog posts on your site. They will likely want to check them out because, as you have pointed out, they are the pages getting the most traffic, and they may want to see what the buzz is all about.

Adding the ability for your readers to search on your site is another way to increase page views. You can set this up through Google and you may even earn additional money when readers conduct searches. Google will serve up some ads when readers do the searches on your blog, and if they click on them you will end up making money (for more on this, see chapter 9). Also, by using the comments section and getting people engaged in a conversation you may keep them coming back to respond and read responses. This too will help to increase page views.

Another option for increasing the amount of time they stay on your blog is to use the blog widget called "LinkWithin." To set it up you simply go to the LinkWithin.com site and sign up. It's easy. Within two minutes you will have this widget set up on your blog. You have probably seen it in action on other blogs and never even realized what it was. It offers posts to readers that coincide with what they are reading. So if someone is reading a post on your blog, they will see three or four little boxes under it with a line that says, "You may also like:" and readers will often click on those pictures to read additional articles.

Although a calendar won't work with all blogs, because it depends on what your focus is, it will work with some. For my local blog I had the idea that an ongoing family-events calendar would increase traffic. My thought was that I could list local family-friendly events on the calendar, and then link each entry to a related blog post (if I had taken the time to write one). I added an inexpensive calendar through KeepandShare.com, which is easy to set up and use. I was right—it instantly at least doubled my monthly page views!

This worked for me because formerly I posted a blog post two to three weeks before an upcoming event. A day or two after I published the post, people would forget about it. But by adding that event to the calendar, and linking it to the blog post page, people can continuously refer back to it as they are looking at the calendar and see the event listed.

These are just a couple of examples of how you can use widgets and other blogging tools to help increase your traffic. They are out there. You just need to see which ones make sense for your blog and will work for you. Many are free, so if they sound like they would work, they are worth giving a shot.

Chapter Eight
Setting Goals, Measuring Success

*"That some achieve great success, is proof to all
that others can achieve it as well."*
—Abraham Lincoln

Determining whether or not your blog has become successful is subjective. There are multiple ways to measure success, or lack thereof, and you will need to determine whether or not it meets your definition of a success. Success will largely be determined by what your initial goals were when you started the blog.

If you started your blog with the intention to promote a product and sell it, and you have achieved that, then your blog was a success. If you started your blog to establish yourself as an expert in a particular area, and you feel you have accomplished that mission, then it is a success. To really determine if your blog is a success, go back to the reason you first started it and see if you have met that mission. If you changed your mission along the way and had a new focus, then determine if that one has been met.

Not everyone starts a blog with the mission of simply making money from it. There are people who have blogs to become experts, share their passion, and provide information, among other reasons.

However, I'm assuming that readers of this book are interested in making a living by blogging; therefore your measure of success is largely going to be determined by how much money you make per month or year. That financial success may not come strictly from your blog, though; it could come from blogging for others, as well as a variety of other routes to earning money as a blogger, which will be discussed in chapter eleven.

DETERMINING GOALS

As with any new project or career path that you take, you will want to set goals. You have probably heard the importance of setting goals before, and some people even take the approach that you shouldn't set goals at all, that you should just wing it. There are supporters on both ends of the spectrum. I tend to be a fan of setting goals, as well as making lists, so that's my advice.

Setting goals helps you determine where it is that you want to be, helps you figure out how you are going to get there, and then gives you a way to measure your success along the way. As you get ready to start your blogging path, pull out your notebook and jot down a few goals. Write down what you would like to accomplish overall, as well as in the next month, six months, and one year.

Your initial goals might look something like this.

Within the next month

- Determine focus of goal and find a URL to use.
- Create the blog layout and design.
- Write and schedule first post.

Within the next 6 months

- Schedule regular blog posts (whether it's on a daily or weekly basis).

- Incorporate some social media and other promotional tools for the blog.
- Begin making money and have realistic expectations about how much money you will be making by blogging up to this point, and throughout the next six months.

When it comes to creating financial goals, you should determine how much money you want, or need, to make, while being realistic. It's not likely that you are going to jump into the blogging world and immediately start making $100,000 per year. But it is plausible that you could establish yourself as a professional blogger and make $40,000 per year. In order to make a good living as a professional blogger, you have to think about making money beyond just writing posts for your own blog. Some people may be able to get away with doing nothing beyond writing posts because they earn enough advertising revenue to pull it off, but most people who want to make a living from blogging will need to expand on that and earn money through additional avenues, such as selling products and services through their blogs, teaching classes, or writing blog posts for clients' blogs. You certainly don't need to do all of these things to earn a living as a blogger, but it's nice to know that there are many options available, so that you can pick and choose which ones interest you and add them to your lineup.

Your financial income will also be impacted by the amount of time that you put into your professional blogging career. If you only dabble in it, don't expect to make much money. If you work at it part time, you can expect to earn a salary that reflects that. If you put a full-time effort into your professional blogging career you should not have any problems earning a living. There are plenty of businesses in need of hiring a good blogger who can help them promote their product or service. The more you know about blogging, and the better you can demonstrate your abilities, the more in demand your blogging services will become. The ability to write professional blog posts that can help clients meet their objectives is a sought-after skill.

It's important to set a realistic timetable when you begin your blogging path. To think that in the first week you are going to make it big is not likely. Not that it can't be done, but if you are like most people you are going to have to work at it and build up your earnings. The important thing is that you keep plugging along and working toward making more money, so that you reach your financial goals. But it is important to go into your professional blogging career with a realistic idea of what you are going to be able to make in the first weeks and months. If you are going to try to make a living only off blogging for your own blog, then it is going to take time to build your blog and brand, acquire advertisers, and make a decent salary. If you immediately take on writing for, or managing, other businesses' blogs, then you should have no trouble making money right off by using your blogging skills.

WORKING TOWARD GOALS

When you first get started, try to stick to having your goals written down, and take stock of them regularly. If you find that you need to alter them, do so. As you learn more about the profession and the direction you want to take, you will no doubt find that you have things you want to include in those goals, or do away with, that you weren't aware of when you first got started. It's a good idea to reevaluate them periodically anyway, so you know which ones you are making, and which ones you want to alter. In the beginning you may want to look at your goals on a weekly or monthly basis. Once your blogging business is up and running and things are humming along, you may only want to set or reevaluate goals once per year.

Personally, I set new writing goals every January 1, and through-out the year those goals are in the back of my mind. Every once in a while throughout the year I will pull out my list of goals, look it over, and make changes if I feel I need to. They help keep me on the right track, but I don't beat myself up at the end of the year if I don't happen to achieve one. My list of goals is certainly flexible, yet I still like knowing that I have given my direction some thought and have an idea of where I'd like to be by the end of the year.

KNOWING YOUR NUMBERS

In order to have a successful blog you will need to get traffic to it, as we have discussed. While we have gone over promoting your blog, so that now you know the myriad things you can do to bring in the readers, it is important to determine if your efforts are paying off. To do this, you will need to know if people are reading your blog. There are multiple ways to do this.

In determining the amount of people who are visiting your site, you can gather statistics from your blogging service provider, for starters. When you log into your account, you should be able to get reports on a daily, weekly, and monthly basis. These reports will give you a snapshot of the number of page views you are getting per day or month. The number of page views does not mean the same thing as the number of visitors. One visitor to your site could look at ten pages, so you don't want to confuse the two statistics. You can also use more in-depth analytic tools that will give you reports showing how people are finding your site, how much time they are spending once they end up there, and more. Analytic tools will also provide you with helpful keywords to use on your blog, as well as ways you can make improvements in order to increase traffic.

The analytic tools may be provided by your blogging service. They may be included in the membership level that you have, or may be offered as an additional add-on service that you will have to pay for to take advantage of. There are also analytic tools, such as Google Analytics, that you can sign up for online or through various marketing agencies that specialize in Internet marketing. If you seek this service from a marketing company it is likely that there will be a fee.

You can learn a lot about your blog traffic just by using a couple of simple tools that are available, which include the reports that your blogging service provider offers. Additionally, you can log on to Alexa.com and type in the web address of any blog. When you do that you will get a snapshot of the amount of traffic that the blog or site is getting. It will give you an Alexa traffic rank, a traffic rank in the United States, and will show you how many sites are linking to yours. As you look over these numbers, keep in mind that the lower the number, the better. For example, the site receiving the most amount of traffic online will be ranked number 1. If you have a few blogs that you read, try typing in their web address just to get an idea of the amount of traffic that they are getting to their site. Compare the sites to see which one is getting more traffic and what their global and U.S. rankings are.

Once your blog is up and running, visit Alexa once a month and type in the address to see where your rank is. If your rank is getting lower, you know your traffic is growing and your blog is headed in the right direction. Keep in mind that there will be some spikes here and there in traffic. When it comes to my local blog there are always traffic spikes around major holidays. I know that people are always looking for event information for Easter, Fourth of July, Halloween, and Christmas. Knowing that people are going to be searching for this information, I make a point to write up an in-depth post providing all the local event details. Those pages always get a lot of views and give me spikes in traffic.

I have identified that I have traffic spikes around the holidays, but you may find that something else gives you traffic spikes. Whether it is a particular topic, a time of year, or something else, if you can identify what it is you can repeat it so that your traffic ranking keeps improving. The more you can give your readers what they want or post what is of interest to them, the more traffic you are going to end up getting to your blog.

When you do the Alexa inquiry you will find that there is also an option to "get details." Although the first page provides a quick snapshot of the site's traffic ranking, you can get a more in-depth look as well. Once you click on the link to get more details, you will be given a site summary of information, and a breakdown of other information, including reach, page views, bounce rate, the amount of time spent on the site, and more. It will even give you an idea of the amount of time it takes for the page to load. The information provided can be helpful in learning more about the traffic to your blog, including the most popular words people are using to find your site, the average age range of visitors, their gender, and more. You will learn some basic information about the demographics of who is visiting your site. Alexa will provide you with some in-depth traffic, keyword, and demographic information and it's free to use. The traffic rank number shown on Alexa is based on the prior three months, so keep that in mind as you are viewing and comparing it.

The information you gather about who is visiting your site and the amount of traffic you are receiving is important. Not only does it help you determine if your blog traffic is growing, but it also shows you where it ranks against others. The information is also helpful when trying to get advertisers to sign up to advertise on your blog. Potential advertisers will want to know how many page views you are getting per month, and they may do a quick Alexa search themselves to verify how popular your blog is.

If you go to Alexa to type in your blog address and find that there is no information, or the volume of information I have described here is not available, don't worry. It's likely that your blog is too new or has not gotten enough traffic yet to start being ranked. Keep working on building the blog, adding quality content, and getting more traffic. As you check back periodically you will likely find that your site does show up in time.

Another site that will give you a little information about the popularity of your blog is Google's Page Rank tool. Just log onto the site, type in the URL of the site, and you will get their "page rank" number. The page rank offers just a number, from 1 to 10, out of 10. For example, you may get a page rank of 2/10, which means that your site does not get all that much traffic. In the case of Google Page Rank you want your blog to have a higher number out of 10. To give you an idea of how difficult it is to have a high ranking on this list, Google is ranked as number one on Alexa, but on Page Rank it only ranks as 9/10. Page Rank shows you how important a page is in the overall scheme of the Internet and it's all based on high-tech algorithms. While it may not give you all the details that Alexa or other analytic tools will, it can still be interesting to see where your blog ranks in terms of importance or popularity on Page Rank.

There are other tools and sites that people use to gather traffic and demographic data as well. Some people like to use the Google AdPlanner to gather information, but it often only provides it for those sites that receive a lot of traffic. Unless your blog has become popular there is a good chance you will not get much info from using this tool.

When it comes to traffic to a blog, some people will take into account such things as the traffic's reach, reader retention rates, and the conversion rate, or the rate that you are getting the reader to do something (e.g., subscribe, click on an ad, buy something, etc.). You may measure your success based on how long you get your readers to visit your site, aiming to take them from fifty-eight seconds to two minutes, or getting them to participate in some other way.

In the beginning you may use a variety of methods to determine your traffic success, but as time goes on you will find that you are partial to one method over another and that some numbers mean more to you than others.

OTHER WAYS TO MEASURE SUCCESS

There are more ways to measure success beyond what your monthly traffic is, your Alexa ranking, or your Google Page Rank. As a professional blogger you will know if you are successful if you are achieving the goals you set and if you feel you are doing what it is that you want to do with your blogging. There is monetary success, which means making the amount of money you want to from your blogging, and there is traffic from your blog. But the two are not necessarily related, especially if you are providing blog post writing services to others. Your personal blog may not get much traffic, or may not have a good ranking, yet you may be making a living as a blogger, because you are working for others.

Another way to determine the success of your blog is by the number of subscribers that you have. Having subscribers means you have an audience, or a platform, and it can help you secure additional money-making opportunities. If you see your blog subscribers increasing, or you are happy with the number of them that you have, then take that into account when determining blog success.

There are some people who take reader commenting as a measure of success for their blog. They find that if they can get numerous people to comment, then it means the blog, or that post, is successful.

You may find this helpful in determining whether people are engaged with what you are posting, but given what was said earlier about comments I would not say that it tells a great deal about the overall success of a blog. However, you may find that it is an aspect that you want to monitor and work at increasing. Familiarity is another measure of success. If people are becoming familiar with your blog and brand, then you are achieving a level of success with your blogging and your promotional efforts. That familiarity may come in the form of mentions by others in the industry, or, if you have a local blog, it may come in the form of people making reference to it while you are out in public. For example, on my local blog, I had promoted a special program for kids that was holding registration. When I showed up to register with my children, there were quite a few people there, and I overheard some of them telling the women they were registering with that they learned about the activity from my blog. I spoke up and let them know that it was my blog they were talking about, and the woman who were registering people said, "I can't thank you enough. We have had so many people register because they learned about the program from your blog." Incidents like that, which happen on a regular basis, let me know that my local blog has become successful in our area.

Monetary success may come from writing blog posts, but as we will learn later on, there are other things you can do to earn money in your professional blogging career. Another way you will be able to determine if your blogging is successful is the additional opportunities that it brings to you. If your blogging is bringing you additional work in blogging for others, opportunities to teach others about blogging, helping you sell products or services, or promoting other money-making options, then your blog is a success. The real measure of a blog's success is whether or not it is suiting the purpose that you created it for. If you refer back to your initial reasons of why you created the blog in the first place, you will recall what it was that you wanted to accomplish. Whether it was to build a platform, earn money, or establish yourself as an expert in a particular area, if you have met that goal, then your blog is a success.

Over time, you should evaluate what is working and not. Everyone once in a while see if there is something better you could be doing on your blog, such as moving around your widgets or advertising. If your advertiser has a contract to be in a specific spot on your blog then you can't move it, but if it's something like Google ads or affiliate ads, try moving them around on the site to see if you get a better response. Periodically look at your blog traffic. Whether you do this weekly or monthly, check out your page views, Alexa ranking, and number of subscribers. See if your audience is growing, and if it had a big surge, take note of what you did differently to achieve that.

It's easy to get caught up in the rankings and numbers when it comes to blogging. We all tend to look at how many people view our pages each day or month, or how much money is generated from advertising, but there is much more that goes into being a successful professional blogger. These things are interesting and can be important, but they are not the only things that matter or the only things you should give your attention to. To really get a picture of how your blog is doing, and to measure its success, look at the bigger picture, rather than only focusing on the numbers.

At the end of the day how you feel about your blogging is the greatest measure of success. If you feel passionate and enjoy what you are doing, that is going to far outweigh the rank number or page views per month. Because if you don't enjoy what you are doing it won't much matter what your traffic rank is. Enjoying being a professional blogger is the most important measure of success you have.

Chapter Nine
Making Money from Blogging

"All that we are is the result of all we have thought. The mind is everything. What we think, we become."
—Buddha

If you want to be a professional blogger then it stands to reason that you will want to make some money doing so. Making a living as a professional blogger is what will afford you the opportunity to continue blogging, rather than having to seek out other employment. There are skeptics out there that may feel people can't make a living as a blogger. To that, I say nonsense!

Professional blogging today is every bit as much of an attainable career and one that can pay your bills as any other. The Internet age we live in today has created many new career fields, most of which a decade or so ago people would have been skeptical that someone could make a living at. Blogging is no different. Just because someone else may not be able to make a living as a blogger, doesn't mean that you can't. It really comes down to getting out of what you put into it, maintaining a positive mindset, and learning everything you can about the profession. These are the same factors that help everyone else to succeed in every other career field.

If you put in the time to learn about the blogging career field, as you are doing reading this book and will continue to do, and you put your skills to work, you will succeed. It's important in any career field you enter that you maintain a positive mindset. If you believe you will succeed at what you are doing, then you will most likely succeed. If you doubt your abilities and your actions in your blogging quest, then you may find it more difficult to overcome challenges. A positive attitude in life is essential to any success. Having said that, let's look at some of the various ways you can make money just on your own blog. We will discuss additional ways you can make money in your blogging career in the next chapter.

STUDY TOP BLOGGERS

We have already taken a look at some popular blogs that are online and thriving. It's a good idea for you to take a couple of hours and just study what successful bloggers are doing. When you view their blogs, try to pick out the various ways that they are making money from their blogs. Do they have advertising? Are they doing paid reviews? Are there other products that they are selling? There are many ways you can make money on your blog, and these are just a few of them. Let's look at the popular blogs that we discussed back in chapter two and take a look at how they are earning money.

- **HuffingtonPost.com**—As mentioned earlier, at one time this blog was reported to be making around $2.3 million per month. They report that they have over 28 million unique visitors to the site each month. One look at the site and you can see that they allow advertising, so their revenue is likely coming from that, combined with the high volume of traffic they get each month.

- **ZenHabits.net**—When you look at this blog you will see that Leo does not have advertising on it, which may come as a surprise to many. But he still earns a living from his blogging career by branching out and selling other items, such as his books and online courses.

- **Mashable.com**—With over 20 million visitors per month, they also offer advertising, which helps them raise millions regularly.

- **Copyblogger.com**—This blog has over 170,000 subscribers and growing. While you won't see ads on this blog, like you do on so many others, there are links to owner Brian Clark's business, Copyblogger Media, where people can purchase his services.

- **TreeHugger.com**—Since this is a blog that is part of the Discovery Channel family, it has advertising, as well as promoting Discovery's other media outlets to their readers.

- **ChrisGuillebeau.com**—This blog sells products, including books written by Chris. He also sells his speaking abilities by offering talks at conferences and other such venues.

- **TechCrunch.com**—This blog gets over 13 million unique visitors each month and they do sell advertising. Their blog states that an advertiser must have an advertising budget of at least $25,000 in order to advertise with them.

- **SethGodin.typepad.com**—Seth's blog is where he keeps in touch with and builds his platform. He's written over a dozen bestselling books, with no indication that he's going to slow down anytime soon. Visitors to his blog have access to purchasing his line of books.

- **PerezHilton.com**—This blog focuses on reporting celebrity gossip. They report that they get 12 million unique visitors each month. They do sell advertising on the blog, as well as promoting their other media outlets, including a radio show.
- **DrudgeReport.com**—This blog, run by Matt Drudge, reports that they get over 13 million unique visitors per month and nearly 800 million page views each month. With advertising as his main source of revenue, there have been newspaper reports that Drudge earns around a million dollars per year from the site.

Selling advertising space on blogs is a common way to go. Most people who have a popular blog offer some sort of advertising opportunity. Those who do not offer advertising only skip it because they have found other revenue-generating options, such as selling books or their services. With your own blog you will want to explore the opportunities that advertising options will provide.

When it comes to getting advertisers for your blog, it is important to realize that you will need to have decent traffic to offer before you are able to secure advertisers. If your site is not getting traffic, there won't really be a reason for potential advertisers to consider placing an ad on your site. If you do have decent traffic to your site, then you should be able to secure advertisers.

Many bloggers use, or have tried using, advertising networks like Google AdWords on their blog. Google AdWords is easy to set up, runs effortlessly, and can generate money for you based on the number of ads that are shown, as well as every time someone clicks on one of the ads. This may be a route you want to explore, especially when you first get started. Once you are getting some good steady traffic to your blog, you can then seek out advertisers who may want to reach your audience. What you charge for that advertising space is up to you, or you can negotiate it with the client.

Don't expect to get rich from Google AdWords. While you can earn a little money here and there per month, it is difficult to earn a lot of money from their platform. You may want to start out using it, and then add in or replace them with advertisers that pay you directly once your monthly traffic has increased. There are other advertising programs that work similarly to AdWords that you can explore. All of these programs simply provide you with a bit of code that you will need to place on your blog, and then the ads will run automatically. You can filter out certain keywords and advertisers, if you want to keep particular businesses or themes off your blog. They also offer the ability to log in each day and month to generate reports showing how much money you have earned. Payments are sent to you automatically, providing you have met the minimum threshold to receive one that month.

You have additional options to earn money from your blog as well, including Commission Junction or ClickBank, where you can sign up, choose the advertisers you want to put on your blog, and then earn a commission from sales that people make. There are also commission opportunities through places like Amazon. com. If you are going to feature books or products on your blog, for example, you may want to create a commission account on Amazon, so that you can link the products and earn a commission off any sales.

Many businesses have commission-based affiliate programs that you can sign up for and add them to your blog. Affiliate programs are an easy way for bloggers to earn money. If you find products and services that you like, take a look at their site to see if they have an affiliate program. If they do, you can sign up, place the ads on your site, and begin earning money. You do not have to have all the links set up as ads either. Adding the affiliate links as part of your content will help to improve the click-through rate and increase the amount of money you earn from them. To do this, you would simply write an informational piece, linking the name of the program with your affiliate link. Also, any time you are writing a post and that company's name comes up, you can hyperlink to the company using your affiliate link.

BLOG DESIGN AND MONETIZING

The blog design and layout you choose can have an impact on the money that you make if advertisers are involved. When it comes to what people read on a blog, or any website, they typically read the page in an "F" pattern. What that means is that they tend to read across the top, down the left side, across the center of the page, and further down the left. Therefore, you want to take this into consideration when setting up your blog. If you are selling a product, or generating revenue from pay-per-click ads, you want to make sure they fit into the "F" pattern on the page in order to maximize revenue.

FINDING ADVERTISERS

If your blog is going to be powered by advertisers, you may be wondering where you are going to find them. Well, in all honesty, if your blog is popular enough, then the advertisers will come to you. When you have a blog that gets millions of visitors per month, potential advertisers are bound to catch word of it and want to be there, too. If you don't get millions of visitors per month you can still get advertisers, you may just need to seek them out.

If you are going to have advertising on your blog, create an "Advertising" page. On that page, offer a little detail about your blog, such as traffic statistics and advertising rate information. Make sure you include a way for those interested in advertising to contact you. Having this information will likely bring you some advertising inquiries as your blog becomes popular. You can also write up an email that contains advertising information, or create a brief media kit, so you can give it out to potential advertisers.

Those who will be interested in advertising on your site are usually those who are trying to reach the same audience that your blog has. If you know your audience well, and you should, then you should not have any problem identifying businesses that would be a good fit for advertising on your blog.

In order to obtain advertisers you will need to have the documents and information available that will help generate that interest. Potential advertisers will want to know what your monthly traffic rate is, for starters. They will also want some rate information and to know where on your blog their ad will be placed. The more information you can provide to them, the better. Your best bet is to create an advertising informational page, where they can view the information when they would like to, and then contact you if they are interested in going forward, or to provide more of a generic advertising page that prompts them to contact you for additional info. Once they do that, you can provide them with a link to the information they need, or a document that contains it. By taking the latter route you will be able to exchange words with them and follow up later on their initial interest.

You are going to end up making more money on your blog if you sell the ad space directly, than if you go with a third-party server to run the ads on your site. And selling the ad space directly is not as difficult as it may seem. Once you have an interested business, be sure to get it in writing what they will get (e.g., how long the ad will run, where it will run, the amount they are paying, etc.). Always get some of the funds up front. If you can, have them pay the entire bill in advance. If they are not willing to do that, get the first month paid ahead, so that they are always paying ahead of time for the advertising.

What you charge for advertising is totally up to you, and what the market is willing to pay. Don't sell yourself short with advertising, but don't price it so high that nobody is interested in taking a shot at signing up with you. If you have competitors, see if their blog provides information on what they charge for advertising so you have something to compare it to. There are multiple ways you can sell advertising space, as well. While you can offer a CPM (cost per thousand), you can also offer a one-time placement, a cost per click, or even a special announcement advertisement. You can get creative with the type of advertising opportunities that you offer, as well as what rate you are willing to accept for it. CPMs are based on the number of times that pages on your blog are viewed, so your CPM cost to advertise on your site would be based on every 1,000 page impressions. For example, if you were charging $50 per CPM, an advertiser would get 1,000 page impressions for their $50.

There are various ad sizes that your advertisers can opt for. A quick online search for banner sizes will give you ads to view so that you can see the sizes and how they would fit in on your blog. You can also offer advertising within your content, and provide a link to their site. Another option is to write content blog posts that are advertising, or advertorials. They appear as though they are editorial in nature, like you are simply telling people about a company, but the blog post has been paid for by the advertiser. Either you can write this type of pay-for-post ad, or the advertiser can write it themselves.

It's important that with any advertising that you take on your site, whether via a content-driven post or a banner ad, that the ads are suitable for your site. For example, you wouldn't want the ads of your competitor, or of a company that you are blogging against, to appear on your site (unless of course you are comfortable with it). But the bottom line is that you should approve of everything and anything that is going on your blog, because it is your reputation and blog that are on the line. It's your job to ensure anything that goes on your blog meets your standards for quality, ethics, and anything else that matters to you.

Your blog is a representation of you (unless you are blogging anonymously, of course), so you want it to be a reflection that you agree with. If an advertiser wants to place a blog post, or advertorial, on your site that you think is poorly written, then you are better off explaining that to the client. If you put up a poorly written blog post, it could reflect on you and do more damage than it's worth. In such a case, if you still wanted the advertiser, you would want to work with them to clean up the blog post so that it meets your quality standards.

My local blog has been designed to be a family-friendly site. Therefore, any advertising that is done on the blog has to fit into that niche. Whether they are run through Google AdWords or from direct advertisers, the ads are ones that families will not mind seeing, and may find helpful. I would not allow ads that didn't fit the family-friendly theme, or they might offend my audience.

GETTING PAID

Once you sell some advertising the fun part comes in, which is getting paid. As you get going it is best to set up a business bank account, and you can link that to PayPal. Advertisers can pay you via PayPal, or by check, as well as by any other method you feel is acceptable. I have been paid numerous times via Western Union for articles I have sold to a magazine in Qatar. I'm usually willing to take the funds just about any way they want to send them, providing it's a legitimate manner.

For Google AdSense and affiliate programs, you will sign up through their site and a check will be sent to you. Some may offer direct deposit arrangements as well. Those advertisers that you handle directly, rather than through an ad server, will pay you directly. You will have to determine your own payment arrangements, but you should get at least the first month up front. I try to get the entire length of the advertising contract up front, so that it's a done deal and I don't have to chase the funds each month. You can write up your own advertising contract for them to sign, which can be as simple as a letter of agreement, stating the terms, amount, and what they will be getting.

If you are hired by a business to write blog posts for them, you have a few options when it comes to being paid. If I have not worked with the business before, I require half of the total amount for the work to be paid up front, with the balance due upon submitting the work. This is a policy you should have for all new clients that you work with, so you don't do a bunch of work and then get stiffed after the work is done. Once you have worked with a client for a while you no longer have to do this if you don't want to. You can always bill after the work has been completed. But in the writing industry, it is standard practice to get half of the funds up front, particularly from newer clients, for work assignments such as writing blog posts.

MERCHANDISE OPPORTUNITIES

As mentioned above, some of the most popular blogs on the Internet sell merchandise, which helps support the blogger. This is an opportunity that every blogger has. Whether you have a product of your own, or you want to sell other people's merchandise on your blog, there are plenty of products that you can sell through your blog to increase revenue.

If you enjoy writing a lot, or if you want to hire a ghostwriter, you can write books and sell them on your blog. Some bloggers even take their blog posts and turn them into a book to sell on the site. There are readers that enjoy being able to get all the most popular posts in one book that they can carry with them and read anywhere. This works for some, but depends on the type of blog that you have. If you are offering timeless information and advice, then this is an option. If, on the other hand, your blog offers event information or celebrity gossip, it would be more difficult to sell that content as a book.

You can also sell shirts, hats, or any other products that you think your audience will be interested in. If you can come up with a product on your own, so that you can make a higher profit from it, as opposed to selling someone else's product, that's even better. Once your blog is popular, you can even sell blog-branded merchandise. There are plenty of companies today that offer the ability to create custom shirts, bags, buttons, and stickers, all of which can easily be sold on your blog.

The ability and options for selling merchandise on your blog are there. You just need to be creative and find the ones that will work to bring in an income for you. Don't think you are tied to one. You can try as many routes to revenue as you would like, so that you can see what will and won't work in helping you earn money from each blog post that you write. This information gives you an idea of some of the various ways that you can earn money from your own blog. Consider the possibilities and determine which ones would work the best for you, or that you would like to get started with first.

BOOK OPPORTUNITIES

As a blogger you are establishing yourself as an expert in a particular area. You are also building a platform. These are two important qualifications that one needs in order to become a successful book writer, at least for nonfiction books. Book-writing opportunities are another revenue-producing opportunity that you will have as a blogger. You can always take some of your blog posts and turn them into a book or e-book, or you can write one that is based on the genre, yet that hasn't yet been covered verbatim on your blog.

Being a professional blogger you will also be able to seek out book-writing opportunities, whether ghostwriting or not, that are based on the topics you are blogging about, or about blogging itself. Having several blogs myself, and being a continuous blogger for a variety of paid clients, has helped me to get additional blogging work and has enabled me to write the book you are reading.

E-books and traditional print books are a possibility for increasing your earnings as a blogger. These publications can easily be sold on your blog, or on the blogs of those you are writing them for. Some people choose to seek out traditional publishers for this, while many others today are handling everything themselves through self-publishing routes. If you are interested in selling your own books and e-books on your blog, be sure to check into the logistics of each route to see which one makes the most sense for you. If you have a large enough platform, or audience, to your blog you shouldn't have a difficult time getting a book contract with a traditional publisher. However, you will also find that you may make more money if you handle the publishing yourself. Be sure to do your homework on this before jumping in, so you know which will be best route for you to take.

ASKING FOR DONATIONS

If you want to be a professional blogger and make a living from doing so, you need to find a way to earn money from your blogging, right? Well, there are some people who ask for donations from their readers. They have a "make a donation" button on their blogs or they may occasionally ask their followers to make a donation. Is there anything wrong with this? The answer to this is highly debatable. There are some people who find it ridiculous and unprofessional to ask for donations, and there are others that see nothing wrong with asking people to cough up a little cash for the content that they read. Personally, while I don't do it, I don't think there's anything inherently wrong with asking for donations.

A newspaper or magazine gets paid not only by the advertisers, but also by the readers who purchase the publication. The books people read have been paid for as well. But when content makes its way to the Internet, everyone assumes it should all be free. The problem is that someone is working hard to produce all that content and they should be, and need to be, paid for their efforts. Just because the content is going online, rather than in a glossy magazine, for example, doesn't mean that it took any less effort to write it up.

If people like the information that they are getting from a blog, or they find it useful in their lives, there's nothing wrong with giving a few dollars per year to support it. A magazine subscription costs around $12 to $14 for the year, so what's wrong with giving your favorite blogger a dollar per month to support what they are doing? Nothing! If asking for donations (or subscription fees) is okay for NPR, PBS, magazines, and all the organizations out there, then there's nothing wrong with asking for donations or a subscription fee from those who use and enjoy your blog on a regular basis.

You can't force people to give, of course, but just asking that they donate a few dollars to you through PayPal if they appreciate the work you are doing is fine. That way you can continue doing your work and they can continue getting the content that they enjoy. While you may come across a couple of people who find it annoying,

125

the majority of people will not mind that you ask them to support what you are doing, and some will in fact donate. Suggesting that readers who can afford it donate a couple of bucks to support your efforts so you can continue to provide the information is not something you want to do often, however. That would only serve to annoy, and possibly chase away, your readers. But done tastefully, a couple of times per year, it should not be a problem, especially if you have built a platform of loyal fans.

On the other hand, if you are making money selling a product or service, you may want to avoid asking for donations. The donations route is better suited to someone that is primarily writing blog posts, without adding on all the ancillary items to sell. If you are selling products and services or your blog is part of a larger business, you may look a bit greedy also seeking donations from your readers. Asking for donations from your readers should be a route you take to support the writing you are doing, especially when you are having difficulty finding other ways to earn money from it. When you know you have a base of people who enjoy what you write, and would not want to see it go away because you need to go get a day job, try the donations route.

Again, if people are willing to pay a dollar per month or more for a magazine subscription it is not out of line to ask them to consider paying you that much for reading your monthly content. While it shouldn't be mandatory, and you don't want to make your readers feel pressured or guilty, it doesn't hurt to put the thought out there and see what happens.

ADDITIONAL PERKS

Once your blog is up and running like a well-oiled machine and monthly page views are increasing, you will find that there are some additional benefits to blogging. Marketers have found that using bloggers is an effective way to get the word out about their products and services. Many intentionally seek out bloggers and offer them free products or services in hopes of getting a review or write-up on their blog. This can be great for you as a blogger, because it means you can have access to a lot of free merchandise and services.

There are bloggers who receive everything from free books and electronics for their reviews to a variety of other products. You may be able to score theme park tickets, hotel stays, restaurant meals, and much more. While these things won't pay your bills at the end of the month, they will give you products and services that your family can use. The only thing that is usually required in exchange is a review of the product or service in question. As a professional blogger, I have received quite a few review items, including books, food, and even kitchen gadgets. I have been offered some that I haven't even accepted, simply because they were something I knew I wouldn't want to use or be interested in finding someone to give it to. In order to help get product and service review opportunities, mention them on your blog. Just have a blurb on the Contact or About page that says you are happy to provide product reviews and can be reached at the following email address. Then the company can contact you there to make arrangements regarding where to send the product or gift certificates for services.

PROVIDING DISCLOSURE

It is important to understand that if you are going to take any products or services, or money, in exchange for a review, that you must follow the Federal Trade Commission (FTC) laws that require you to provide disclosure of this. The guidelines set forth by the FTC pertain to bloggers, as well as advertisers and celebrity endorsements. In 2009 these guidelines were updated to reflect the new changes, as they hadn't been updated since 1980.

These new guidelines have changed some things for bloggers. Prior to these guidelines bloggers would take all these free products and services and would usually give glowing reviews in return. The problem was that their audience didn't realize that they gave the glowing review or endorsement in exchange for the free product, or the payment they received to provide the review.

The FTC has specifically stated on its website that:

> *The revised Guides specify that while decisions will be reached on a case-by-case basis, the post of a blogger who receives cash or in-kind payment to review a product is considered an endorsement. Thus, bloggers who make an endorsement must disclose the material connections they share with the seller of the product or service.*

What this means for you as a blogger is that if you receive a product, service, gift certificate, or payment in exchange for a review or endorsement on your blog you will need to disclose that information to your readers. You will need to include a disclosure statement that lets your readers know you received the product for free in exchange for the review, or that you were paid to provide the review. This is the case if you are personally sharing your experience with the product, rather than it merely being an advertisement for the product or service.

Don't let this FTC guideline scare you away from all the products, services, and even entertainment that you can take advantage of by being a blogger. It's one of the great perks of being a blogger! In time, your blog will be tapped for conducting reviews and if it's something you are interested in, you should go for it. All you need to do when you write up that blog post that provides your personal review is to state that you were given the product, or entertainment tickets, to try out. You are just letting your reader know that you didn't buy the product, or whatever it is. You were given the item and that it was in exchange for the blog post you are writing, or recording, if it's a vlog.

What that would look like in your blog post is simple and after a while you will write it without giving it much thought. Your audience may not even give it much thought either as they read over your review, but you must have it there in order to avoid getting into any legal hot water with the FTC. Here are a few examples of ways that you can word your disclosure in your blog post:

> *After receiving a review copy of the new book . . .*
> *I was offered four tickets for my family to try out this theme park for the day . . .*
> *I got this new product in the mail to try and here are my thoughts . . .*

Providing that little tidbit of information to your readers, to let them know you didn't actually go buy what it is that you are reviewing, takes seconds and will keep you from getting into any legal problems. The FTC has created such guidelines for bloggers to try to keep things more honest and fair. Your readers trust you and what you are writing, or at least they should, so you don't want to violate that trust by personally encouraging them to purchase something or telling them a product or place is great when you're only doing so because you were given the item or experience for free. If you receive anything in exchange for providing a personal review or endorsement of a product, place, or service, then you need to be honest with your readers and let them know that. This only pertains to those blog posts that provide a personal account of your experience with something that you were given for free or were paid to try or to write a favorable personal review about.

To take disclosures a step further, many bloggers add a blanket disclosure statement to their blog. You can do this on the About page, or even as a small note in the margin or at the bottom of posts that contain the reviews in question. Just a simple message to the effect that you do at times take products in exchange for a review will further help protect you, but you still need to add the disclaimer into the blog post where you are writing about the personal experience or review in question.

Chapter Ten
Additional Money-Making Opportunities for Bloggers

"We are what we repeatedly do. Excellence, therefore, is not an act, but a habit."
—Aristotle

In the last chapter we went over the various ways that you can make money on your blog. But being a professional blogger doesn't mean that you are bound to only making money from your own blog. Not at all! In fact, there are some professional bloggers who make more money blogging for other people and doing a variety of other things outside of their blog than they make from the blog itself.

Think of your blog as your home base. If you are going to make money outside of it, but that income is mainly a result of your being a blogger or having your own blog, then all of your other blog-related tasks are just avenues you can explore leading off of your home base. You keep coming back to your blogging, and you maintain that it's an important and steady facet of your business, but it is a springboard for all the other revenue-generating opportunities that may come your way.

THINKING BEYOND THE BLOG

As mentioned previously, being a professional blogger establishes you as an expert, both at blogging, as well as in whatever your niche or topic is. When you start thinking beyond the pages and posts of your blog, you will find that there are a whole lot of opportunities to make money as a professional blogger. Most of the time people think of only writing their own blog posts in terms of making a living as a blogger, and then they begin to question if it can really be done. No matter what type of career field you enter, there are likely going to be times that you are doing work for someone else in order to make money.

Blogging for yourself, on your own blog, may be liberating in that it gives you the freedom to do what you'd like, when you want to do it. But relying only upon writing your own blog posts to make a living may make it more challenging. That's not to say that it can't be done, because if you can get enough traffic to your blog then it certainly can happen. Most of the popular blogs we have already discussed do exactly that—they make money off of what they do right on their own blogs. But for those who want to consider the field outside of their own blog posts, there are plenty of money-making opportunities.

Here are some of the additional ways you can make money having a career as a professional blogger.

- **Writing and ghostwriting blog posts for others.** There are a lot of opportunities to do this. The number of blog-writing opportunities that are out there increases all the time. People create blogs and hire bloggers to write the posts. Businesses see the value in blogging as a way to bring in traffic to their site, promote their products and services, and keep in touch with their customers. They often hire bloggers to do the work for them. While some hire bloggers to work in-house and be on the payroll, most simply offer work-for-hire arrangements, so you can do it on a freelance basis. SEO blog post writers are in hot demand. There are plenty of companies out there willing to hire someone to create a batch of SEO blog posts for them, maintain their blog, or write for them on a weekly or monthly basis. There are plenty of magazines and newspapers today that offer blogs, and they hire bloggers to contribute. Some of the opportunities that come your way will provide you with a byline, so that your name is given as the writer, but many do not. I write blog posts on a weekly basis for a variety of clients and it is all ghostwriting. I write the blog posts based on ideas or angles they prefer, and they pay me for them, but my name is not associated with the posts. Nobody knows that I wrote them. Some people don't care for that, because they want their name associated with their writing. But the sooner you can let go of having to have your name attached to everything, the more money you will likely be able to make as a professional blogger. There is a lot of money to be made in ghostwriting for blogs. At the end of the day it is the payments from writing those posts that are going to pay your bills, not the fact that your name is listed as the author.

- **Writing articles and books about blogging.** This was mentioned earlier, but once you establish yourself as a professional blogger and have some experience at it, you can use that to write about the act of blogging itself. You can write and sell articles and books. The opportunities in this area range from ghostwriting and writing for others to doing it for yourself. Articles can include those used online, as well as in print publications. Selling an article on a blogging topic to a magazine, for example, can also be helpful in driving traffic to your blog, if they allow you to add the name of your blog in your bio line. The more you do this the more you will be establishing yourself as a professional blogger. With that, your chances of being able to do some of the following income-generating opportunities should be even greater.

- **Writing articles and books about your niche area.** This is similar to above, only instead of the work focusing on the topic of blogging, it would cover the genre that your blog covers. Your blog establishes you as an expert in the area that your blog topic covers. You can also write books and e-books in that same genre as a way to increase your salary, whether on a ghostwriting or bylined basis.

- **Creating additional blogs.** As a professional blogger you can be a serial blogger. Some of the blogging software companies will allow you to have multiple blogs for one price, while others offer all the blogging you want for free. Creating multiple blogs is a way for you to test out a variety of subjects you are interested in blogging about to see what works and what doesn't. If you find some of your blogging ideas help generate an income, and others don't, then you should ax those that don't help you make money or assist you in reaching your goals. Focus on those that make you money, or bring you money-making opportunities, and create more that interest you or that you feel can be used to make money.

- **Managing other company blogs.** As mentioned, many businesses today hire bloggers to manage their blogs, even on a freelance basis. If you can secure one of these positions, you can negotiate a weekly or monthly rate for taking care of their blog. This will help you to generate a monthly income.

Actively seek out a dozen of such clients or more and you can be generating a nice additional portion of your yearly salary as a professional blogger. When managing another business's blog, they often give you the log-in information and you simply log in and handle everything. Other companies prefer you to write the blog posts and submit them to someone within the company, and they personally put them up on the blog.

- **Creating and selling blogs.** This is another opportunity for those who enjoy getting blogs started and then don't mind handing them off to others. You can build a blog to become popular, have a lot of monthly page views and subscribers, and then sell it (like Arianna Huffington did). Or you can also get paid to create new blogs for companies. Being able to take a blog from idea to reality and knowing all the steps to get it there is a marketable skill that will get you hired.

- **Providing blog consulting services.** Once you have established yourself as an expert, you can begin offering blog consulting. There are people and businesses that would like the benefit of a blog, but don't want to hire a ghostwriter or take the time to read through books to figure out how to do it. As an established professional blogger you can provide your services, information, and advice to those who need it. Consulting services can be helpful in coaching other freelancers, as well as providing businesses with the information they need to get their blog up and running, or to make it more effective. Being able to understand the analytics and what goes into creating and maintaining a successful blog is important information, and businesses are willing to pay you to share it with them and walk them through the process.

- **Offering speaker opportunities.** Sure, speaking can be a tough one for those who fear standing before a crowd and sharing what they know. But if you can get over your fear of public speaking, you can share your blogging expertise through speaking opportunities. These gigs, by the way, will help add to your yearly salary, and further build your platform, establish you as an expert, and help you network. As you network you may find additional companies to which you can offer your consulting and blog writing services. Speakers are hired at a variety of venues, such as business, writing, and blogging conferences, and at other related events.
- **Teaching classes.** There are plenty of other people who are interested in learning the ins and outs of blogging. As a professional blogger, you are in a prime position to teach classes on the subject. There are opportunities for teaching these classes online, or right in your own community. Contact your community center and inquire about offering the class. Attendees will pay for the classes, which you would offer on a weekly basis, usually for an hour or two per week for around six weeks. Many people are interested in these classes, including those looking to blog for fun or profit, and businesses that would like to start reaping the benefits of having a blog. This also provides you with additional means of networking, which could lead to private consulting, as well as blog post writing and management.

As you can see, the ability to earn a living from your professional blogging career is only limited by your imagination and reach. There are plenty of income-generating opportunities out there for the person who is determined, eager, and business minded. With the right mindset as a professional blogger, success is within reach.

Now is the time to pull out your notebook and ask yourself of all the many opportunities that are out there, which can you see yourself doing? If you are not someone who can ever see yourself being a speaker at a conference and telling others about the benefits of blogging, don't worry about it. There are so many opportunities that it's okay to leave that one for someone else while you take on another route. It's all up to what you feel you can, and will, want to do in your quest to make a living as a professional blogger.

FINDING WORK

Now you have an idea of the variety of opportunities that are out there for making money and putting your blogging skills to work. But you may be unsure where to find those clients who are willing to pay you to write blog posts, e-books, or do consulting. This is something that will actually go both ways. You will end up seeking out some of this business on a regular basis, but some of these clients will find you and contact you with their interest in hiring your services.

On your blog you may want to set up a page about hiring your services, and list what services you offer. You can have this on a separate Services page or Hire Me page, or you can have it on the About or Contact page. The page you have it on isn't as important as the fact that you have it available so that people realize you offer these services.

Alternatively, or in addition to this, you can set up a business website for your services. Your business website would tell about your business, which is professional blogging services, and would establish you as an expert blogger and explain the variety of blogging and blogging-related services that you offer. Keep in mind that your blog and business website, if you have one, are reflections of you and your work. Therefore they should always look professional and read well. When businesses see your blog or website, they assume that is the kind of work they will get if they hire you—so keep it neat, professional, and show them what you are capable of.

There are other ways to get blogging and blogging-related work as well. Make some business cards that explain you are a professional blogger, and hand them out whenever you are networking. Other ways to find these opportunities include online job sites, classified ad sites, and advertising.

As you find projects and are offered jobs, you will come across some people who want you to write for next to nothing. I've seen ads where people want to hire bloggers who will write 400-word posts for 50 cents or $1 each. The problem with this is that there are always people willing to do it. Avoid work like this if you are serious about being a professional blogger and want to earn a living. Taking on something like this would be a ridiculous waste of your time. Your time will be better spent finding higher-paying work, writing posts for your own blog, and finding other blogging-related, income-producing activities.

DETERMINING RATES

Speaking of rates, one of the most common questions that people have about blogging for others is how much they should charge. When it comes to blogging for others, people usually pay a flat rate per post or for managing the blog each week or month. You should have an hourly rate in mind that you would like to make in order to feel good about what you are doing and comfortable with the amount of money you will be paid. Keep that hourly rate in mind, but if at all possible don't quote an hourly rate when trying to secure the work. Hourly rates, although some clients think they want them, scare a lot of potential clients. They see a rate that is often higher than they imagined they would pay for a blogger, and they run in the other direction.

The best way to quote a project is to keep that hourly rate in mind that you want to make, then use it to determine a flat rate to quote to the client. To do this you need to know a little about your work speed and habits, so you can calculate the amount. For example, if you know you want to earn $50 per hour and someone asks you to write ten blog posts that are 400 words each, you can calculate to get the amount to quote the person. Assuming you know how long it takes you to write a 400-word article, just multiply that by the number of blog posts you will be writing, and then multiply by your hourly rate, to get the flat rate you would charge. For example, if it takes thirty minutes to write each blog post at that length, then the flat fee would come out to $250 for writing the ten blog posts. You can figure this out by multiplying 0.5 hours per post x 10 posts x $50 per hour = $250 flat fee. Just use that formula, plugging in the time you would spend on each post and desired hourly rate, in order to get the total fee you would charge for the writing.

Quoting someone a flat fee is usually much easier for the client to take and understand than it is to quote an hourly fee. It's also much easier on you. This way you don't have to watch the time it takes you to write them and then try to bill accordingly. Instead, you can work at your own pace and still get paid your flat rate even if you finish them quicker than originally thought or if you take longer to do so.

When it comes to what to charge for services you are offering, you will need to do a little research to find the going rate. You don't want to be the highest rate on the block, but you don't want to be the lowest either. Charge what you believe you are worth and what the market will pay, making sure not to sell yourself short. You can make a living as a professional blogger. There is no reason to come across as desperate or give yourself a ton of work to do for peanuts.

Professional bloggers charge a professional rate they are comfortable with and produce professional work.

TRACKING YOUR EXPENSES AND INCOME

Assuming you are going to make money as a blogger, you will need to file and pay taxes on those earnings. Pick up an accounting software system that will let you easily keep track of income earned and expenses. You can enter payments received and money spent. This will also let you create reports to see where you are at and compare each year to see your growth. It also makes things a lot easier when it comes time to file your taxes. You can print off the report that shows your gross income, expenses, and net income.

As you begin making more money you may find that you need to pay your taxes quarterly, based upon your prior year's earnings. If you are unfamiliar with how this works, speak with an accountant or contact the IRS for clarification. Typically you will get a voucher that requires you to pay taxes four times throughout the year. The taxes you pay each time are calculated off your prior year's earnings. Not only does the IRS like this once you start earning a salary, but it makes it easier for you as well. That way you are not hit with one big tax bill come April on everything you earned over the prior year.

Chapter Eleven
Growing Your Business

"Drive thy business, let not that drive thee."
—Benjamin Franklin

You already read in the previous chapter that if you want to succeed as a professional blogger, you need to think of it as a business. As a professional blogger, someone who is going to make a living from your blogging and blogging-related efforts, you are a business. The sooner you begin thinking of yourself as having a small business, the sooner you will make better decisions (such as not writing for free, as businesses don't usually give away much of their product).

When you think of your efforts as a business, you will also be in a position to think about growing your business. Nearly every successful business in America has someone, or a team of someones, behind it deciding which direction to take it, how to get there, and the best way to overcome any challenges they may come across. In your business, you are that driving force.

BENEFITS OF BUSINESS

Most bloggers start out as freelancers, just doing their thing, selling their services, and conducting business as a freelance professional.

That works for a while, but as you begin to grow, you may find that there are some benefits of becoming a business, rather than continuing on doing your work as a freelancer. When freelancers are ready to take the next step, they often establish a business in the form of a limited liability company (LLC).

Some of the benefits of becoming a business include:

- a limited personal liability for the debts and actions of the company. What this means for you is that if your company were to get into any kind of legal troubles, such as debt or other liability issues, you would not personally be held responsible. Your company would be targeted, but your personal name and assets would not be.
- tax breaks, in that you can deduct quite a few items that you may need to purchase. Everything from your business office supplies to your blogging conferences can qualify for a tax deduction.
- respect. As a company you will find that many people tend to respect what you do and take it more seriously. As a freelancer people often get the idea that you are just dabbling in blogging, but as a business owner they know you are a serious professional in your field.

You will need to check with your state to determine your options. If you are not ready to become an LLC, but you want to use a business name, or a name other than your own first and last one, you will need to file with your state. Depending on what state you live in this is usually either called a "fictitious firm name" or a "doing business as (DBA)" registration. It is inexpensive to file, usually around $50, and it is good for multiple years. Filing an LLC costs a little more, but comes with the benefits of doing so.

Whether you are going to use your own name for your business, file a DBA, or become an LLC, you will want to avoid using your personal social security number for your work. Instead, file for an employer identification number (EIN) if you will be using a DBA or LLC that you can hand out to the people you work for.

Many companies you work for will request your tax identification number, or your social security number, to conduct business. This way they can issue you a tax report when it's time, and you will need to file it with your taxes. The problem is that, as a freelancer, if you don't obtain a separate tax identification number, you will be emailing and faxing your social security number to your contacts at hundreds of businesses, many of whom you will never meet face to face. If you know anything about identity theft, you can see why this could be problematic. To avoid it, visit the website for the Internal Revenue Service (IRS) and file for an employer identification number. They will issue you a number that will be associated with you, that you can give out to all the businesses that you work with that request it for tax purposes.

There are businesses online that you can pay to file all these things for you, such as filing to obtain the tax number. But you do not need to pay someone to take care of that for you. That is something you can file yourself right at the IRS website. Also, check directly with your state's business department for the rules and filing requirements to file any type of business documents. You should be able to file directly right at their site, or through the mail, saving money from paying someone else to file for you. You will also likely need the tax ID number and legal business name to open a business bank account.

If your business will be home based, you can also take advantage of certain tax deductions for your home office. Your home office, which has to be a dedicated room for conducting your business, can be used as a tax deduction. All you need to do is determine the square footage of the home office space and calculate to find out what percentage of your home the office makes up. For example, if your home office is 100 square feet and your home is 1,000 square feet, then your office is 10 percent of your home. That means you should be able to deduct 10 percent of your monthly mortgage, electricity bill, and other expenses for running that office. Be sure to check with the IRS guidelines in this area, or speak with an accountant, so that you get the most up-to-date information and guidelines regarding home office deductions.

GROWING YOUR BUSINESS

There is a lot of advice out there on how to grow a business. So while this book isn't going to go in-depth on this topic, you will want to focus on growing your business once you have it up and running. You can set small goals each month that will help you grow and reach the next level. What your "next level" is will vary among businesses. Perhaps you want to grow the number of subscribers you have, the number of page views per month, or the amount of money you earn per week. This is what you will want to determine, set goals for yourself, and then strive weekly to take steps toward meeting those goals.

Here are just a few ways that as a blogger you can grow your business.

- Ask for referrals from those you work for. If you write blog posts for a company and they are happy with your work, ask them to refer you to anyone they know that may also be able to benefit from a good blog.
- Keep your costs in mind and try to keep them to a minimum. Overhead can often be a real drag for small businesses,

because they spend so much that it's difficult to overcome that number and end up with a decent salary at the end of the month. Especially during your first year, try to keep expenses to a minimum.

- Take a look at what you are doing with your social media, or what you are not doing. If you haven't tapped into using something like Facebook to promote your blog and get the word out about it, give it a try. You have nothing to lose but the little bit of time you put in to create the page.

- If your blogging business is getting a lot of work, you can always hire another blogger to work for you. To avoid taking on a lot of unnecessary expenses, you will want to start out doing this by hiring a freelancer or other individual blogger such as yourself. Essentially, you would be bringing in the work, assigning some blog post writing to the other blogger, and making a cut off the work that person does. By expanding your team you are able to make additional money, without having to do more work. You will, however, need to take caution that you hire a quality writer to give the work to, because your reputation will be on the line. Likewise, you can bring in additional bloggers to write on your own blog. *The Huffington Post* is an example of a blog that hires a wide variety of people to write posts.

There are many ways that you can harness the power of advertising, marketing, or public relations (PR), in order to grow your business. You just need to determine which route is going to be the best one for you to take and which one will be the most economical. While you don't want to focus solely on the amount of money you are spending, you do want to make sure you get the most bang for your buck. Choose those efforts that are going to

145

pay off and get you the exposure you need, even if it costs a little more.

MARKETING AND PROMOTING YOUR BLOG

As you can imagine, not much is going to happen if you don't do anything to market or promote your blog. In addition to writing good content, you need to let people know that your blog exists. Getting the word out is what is going to help drive traffic to your site and bring you the multitude of other opportunities that have been discussed.

There are a lot of creative ways that you can get the word out about your blog. One of the best ways, and also the most cost effective, is through word-of-mouth advertising. If you have an attractive blog that people enjoy reading, they will inevitably pass the link and name of it on to others. They will want to get the word out for you. But there are additional ways to get your blog noticed as well. Keep in mind that some methods may come with a cost, but it is important to choose the ones that will provide you with a good return on investment (ROI).

Here are some options you can consider for helping to get your blog known to the masses.

- **Advertising.** This is a route that many businesses take, because it often works to get people familiar with your name and brand. However, in the quest to help keep your expenses manageable, you really have to consider the possible ROI before plunking down the money to advertise. Some advertising can be quite expensive. Before signing any lengthy contracts for advertising, if you are interested in trying it, go for a short-term trial run to see what type of response you get. Some of the places you would consider advertising your blog include search engines, publications covering topics related to your genre, and even targeted Facebook ads.

- **Press releases.** These can be effective tools when used correctly. It's important that you know how to correctly write and use a press release in order to get a good return on it. Research and learn how to write a professional press release if you don't already know how to do so. Use press releases in order to announce the new blog, news, and milestones. There are many angles that can be used in a press release and they can gain you some media attention, and used online they can help drive traffic to your blog. Not sure what to write a release about? Consider such things as subscriber milestones, new design of the blog, speaking at a conference, celebrating your blog's first year online, etc. Press releases can be released online, as well as sent to local media outlets. If sending online, always copy and paste the text into the body of an email rather than sending it as an attachment. This is usually preferred by editors because they are leery of opening up attachments from those they don't know, fearing computer viruses, and may simply delete your email. If you send the press release in the body of an email, the editor can quickly read it without having to worry about downloading attachments.

- **Sponsorships.** Look for opportunities to sponsor an event that will be attended by your target audience. If you have a blog on fitness or running, for example, get involved in sponsoring races. There are often inexpensive sponsorship opportunities that will get your business card or small flyer into the hands of each of the runners.

- **Speaking opportunities.** Conferences take place around the country on a regular basis. There are conferences geared toward all types of writers, bloggers, and businesses. Beyond conferences, there are venues where you can offer talks on blogging. Other writers and those looking to start blogging would want to hear your advice on blogging, once you are established and are successful in the field. Businesses interested in starting a company blog, or learning how blogging can benefit them, may also be interested in listening to you. All of these are opportunities to share your expertise, hand out business cards, and help to promote you, your blog, and your blogging skills.

- **Teaching classes.** Once you know the ins and outs of being a blogger, you can pass that knowledge on to others through teaching classes and holding workshops. You can either do this online, or you can contact local community centers and see if you can set up a class there. People are willing to pay for classes that cover the information they need. You can offer a four- or six-week course where the attendees pay one flat fee and attend for two hours each week, for example. Another option is to hold one-day seminars or workshops, where you teach blogging skills to businesses. Charging a fee for each participant, you can rent a conference room in a hotel and hold the one-day class there.

- **Guest blogging.** Writing a blog post here and there for someone else's blog, or guest blogging, can be a good way to promote your own blog. You would want to make sure that the blog will reach the audience you are after, and that the blog post covers a topic complementary to your blog and theirs. You also want to make sure that you are doing this for a blog that is actually going to get you traffic. If the blog does not get much traffic, then it could be a waste of time. You need to take that into consideration in deciding if you want to do a guest blog post. If you do guest blog, your work should have a link to your blog in exchange for the post.

- **Social media.** It has been mentioned, but using social media to promote your blog can be quite effective. Learn about the best ways to go about using Facebook, Twitter, Pinterest, YouTube, and others, in order to get the most out of the time you put into it. These outlets give you a way to interact with your audience, as well as for them to share things you post, and be seen by those who may be viewing their activity.

- **Link building.** The more external links you have coming into your blog, the better. It will help your blog to have a better organic search ranking. If you can get some external sites to link to your blog, it will help with promotion. If you write blog posts, or can leave quality feedback comments on other people's blogs or in forums, this should provide you with an opportunity to build links to your blog.

- **Directories.** Depending on the focus of your blog, there are directories that create a database of blogs. You may want to add your blog to the database. Technorati is one, but there are others as well. Some list all types of blogs, while others focus on one particular subject, such as veganblogs.org, which is filled with links to vegan blogs.

- **Sharing.** Giving your readers the ability to instantly share what they have just read is a helpful and effective promotional tool. By adding buttons to the bottom of your blog post, you can allow them to easily post the page on Facebook or Twitter, re-blog it, pin it on Pinterest, Digg it, and more. The great thing about these handy buttons is that you don't have to set it up each time you add a blog post. All you need to do is set it up once to run, and it will automatically be added into the footer of every blog post you publish. Blog hosting sites such as Typepad make the setup process easy by making this one of the "sharing" options offered in the blog settings area.

- **Print efforts.** There are some print marketing efforts that can pay off in helping to get your blog name and address out there. Professional business cards, postcards, or small flyers can be effective tools, and yet they are quite cost effective. For around $20 you can have 200 or more business cards, which can be given out at meetings, handed out when networking or meeting new people, or put on bulletin boards. Creating these products is simple. You can do it yourself online at sites like Vistaprint.

- **Others.** There are many other simple, and even free, ways to promote your blog. You can tell people about it, add a link to it in your email signature line, or ask your subscribers to share it with someone they know. It's also a good idea to make sure you set up your blog with Feedburner so that it is easily distributed, and that your blog is "pinging" to popular search engines every time you publish a post. Pinging sends out a message to a server that lets it know you have published new content. You can get your blog easily listed for this through Google just by going to their blogsearch.google.com/ping page and entering your blog website address. They will take it from there. Once it is indexed in their search engine, your blog will notify their server each time you have published new content.

There are many options out there to help you, or that tout that they will do the job, but it comes down to seeing what works for you. No matter which route you take to help promote your blog you should pay attention to the results. This is the only way you will know where you are getting a good ROI, so that you don't simply throw your money away. Find out which things work, and which ones don't, so that you can focus more of your efforts on the routes that are paying off.

One of the most effective ways to get people to notice your blog is to provide quality content, have an attractive design and layout, and to use SEO keywords to help readers find your blog when they are searching. When you concentrate on these three main things, and then add in a few of the other methods, you shouldn't have any trouble building an audience and increasing traffic to your site.

On another note, there are some things that may not be effective, or may even get people upset with you. This is especially true if you automatically add people to your email subscription list and start sending them marketing emails. People have come to despise spam and hit the delete key without reading it, and if you are identified as a spammer you can actually be in trouble with the law, since it's now illegal to spam people (even though you will notice your in-box is still being hit with lots of spam). Always have permission to send people marketing emails, either by them signing up directly at your site, or by obtaining an opt-in marketing email list of contacts. An opt-in marketing list is one that contains the contact information for people who have indicated that they wouldn't mind receiving offers and messages from companies. You may be familiar with this if you have ever registered for something and were asked whether you would give the company permission to share your info with select partners. If you indicated yes, then your name may have ended up on an opt-in marketing list. These lists can be purchased from companies, even giving the person doing the advertising the ability to narrow their audience down using such information as zip code, age, and gender. If you do send emails out to an opt-in marketing list, avoid sending them too frequently, and always give people a way to unsubscribe if they would prefer to do so.

KNOWING YOUR AUDIENCE

In order for any marketing to be effective and bring people to your blog, you have to know who your audience is. If you have a blog reviewing automobiles, it doesn't make a lot of sense to advertise your blog on a site that specializes in celebrity gossip. You have to know who it is that you are trying to reach, so that you can make an informed decision about what marketing efforts to use, and where to use them, in order to reach those people.

Here are some questions you need to ask yourself when it comes to determining which route you should take for marketing your blog.

- Who are the people that make up my blog's audience?
- Where would I go to find those people, whether online or not?
- Do I have any money to spend marketing my blog or do I need to stick with all of the free routes? If you have some money to invest in your blog, then do it. But don't invest money until there is actually something there for people to read. Focus first on getting a good amount of content, so that when people visit the blog they like what they see.
- What is it that I want to achieve from my marketing? Is it to get more subscribers, increase page views, sell products, etc.?

Your first mission in having your blog is to get it set up, turn your focus to creating content, and then promote it to the masses. You certainly don't want to start out putting your time and effort into marketing when you haven't yet dedicated the time necessary to building a good blog that gives people a lot of quality content to read once they get there. On the other hand, if your blog is great when you do get readers there, then they will want to come back again and again, or subscribe so they don't miss your posts. That's what you want—to attract new followers to your blog, but to keep them as you continue to acquire more.

Chapter Twelve
The Blogging Community

"Everything you want is out there waiting for you to ask.
Everything you want also wants you.
But you have to take action to get it."
—Jack Canfield

As a professional blogger it's a good idea to get to know other blog-gers. It provides a good way to learn more, keep up on trends, and share ideas. There's a good chance that you will not be focusing on the same genre or subject, so you don't have to worry about competi-tion. But even if you are, it should still be just fine. There's enough people in the country and world that there are room for multiple blogs covering the same topics.

There are a variety of ways you can get involved in the blog-ging community, since you will be considered to be a part of the "blogosphere." There is a whole world of bloggers out there, and you can become an active part of that community. You can choose to get involved as little or as much as you'd prefer, but before you decide against getting involved you should at least consider a few of the opportunities and whether or not you could get anything from them. Just being able to network and bounce ideas off other bloggers may be an enriching experience for you and one that you want to take part in.

COMMUNITY OPTIONS

With a little searching around you will find that there are blogging groups you can join. Check places such as Yahoo! Groups and Meetup. com to find those that are online, as well as those that meet in person. A quick online search will also return a list of results that include various blogging associations, unions, and professional groups, such as the Association for Food Bloggers, the Professional Bloggers Association, Independent Theater Bloggers, and the Mom Bloggers Club, just to name a few. Take a few minutes to investigate some of them to see if you feel they will provide you with benefits that make it worth joining. Some may provide helpful blogging tips, help keep you up on blogging trends, and connect you with news and information you can use to become a better blogger and learn more about the area.

By joining some blogging groups you are bound to meet some people to network with. But don't let it stop there. You may also want to consider joining some business-related groups as well. By joining business groups you will learn more about running a successful business, as well as find possible people to sell your blogging services to. Always attend business-oriented meetings with business cards in hand, as well as ready to take them from others, so you can make new contacts and possibly get more paid blogging work.

If you start to look around for a blogging group in your area, or online, and you can't find one that is of interest to you, start your own. Starting your own blogging group is easy and gives you the creative control to have it be geared toward what you want to focus on. If you want a blogging group that meets once a week or month and talks about trends, challenges, marketing, or anything else, you can do that. You can always set the group up on a site like Meetup.

com, which charges a monthly fee, or create a group on Facebook, which is free to use.

In addition to joining blogging groups, you may also want to consider joining groups that are focused on your particular genre. For example, if you blog about astrology, you can benefit from joining a blogging group, but you can also benefit from joining an astrology group. Both groups will give you networking opportunities and help keep you learning all you can about new trends in your area of expertise.

Beyond blogging groups, you may also be able to network and bounce ideas off of other professionals in forums. By finding forums about your topic, or that focus on blogging, you can pose questions, get answers, and read what others are saying about what they are encountering. You will keep up on trends, learn how to overcome challenges, and see that other bloggers are likely going through some of the issues you are encountering.

ATTENDING CONFERENCES

If you have never attended a conference before, you should make it a goal to attend at least one each year. Choose one near your home if you need to, in order to keep travel costs down. Conferences usually have leaders in the field who offer seminars, classes, or talks about a specific topic. If you attend a blogging-specific conference you may find that some of the topics covered include:

- search engine optimization (SEO)
- blog marketing
- defining and reaching your audience
- networking skills
- protecting your work
- using photos on your blog
- earning money with your blog

- essential plug-ins
- ask-the-expert segments
- expert panel discussions
- writing effective blog posts
- mobile blogging
- advertisements and endorsements
- moving your blog
- vlogging
- turning your blog into a book
- building your media kit
- using social media tools
- copyrights and trademarks
- the business side of blogging

This is just a sample of the many topics that may be covered at blogging conferences. Attending the sessions gives you an in-depth look at each topic, which should be taught by an established professional in the field. When you are looking at conferences to attend, avoid just looking for ones that are specifically called "blogger" conferences. You should also take a look at writers' conferences to see if they will be having any sessions that focus on blogging, as many of them do.

The good news about blogging conferences is that there are many options out there and something for everyone. There are all-encompassing blogging conferences, which are geared to all bloggers, and there are some that are geared more toward specific areas or genres in blogging. Here's a sample of what you can find in the area of blogging conferences.

- Wine Bloggers' Conference
- BlogHer Conference
- Minnesota Blogger Conference

- International Food Bloggers Conference
- Beer Bloggers Conference
- Fitness & Health Bloggers Conference
- SocMed & Blogging Conference
- Fashion and Beauty Blogger Conference
- Mommy Blogger Conference
- Women Blogger Conference
- Vegan Bloggers Conference
- Central Florida Bloggers Conference
- Pet Blogging and Social Media Conference

This is just a small portion of the possible conferences for bloggers that take place. But it gives you an idea of the range of possibilities that exist. It doesn't even touch upon the many writers' conferences that offer sessions and speakers on blogging, or all the business-related conferences that may cover blogging for businesses.

In addition to networking and meeting other bloggers and possible clients at conferences, you will also likely learn more about your career field, have fun, and you may score some free merchandise. Many people walk away from conferences with freebies that they can try and then blog about. Just be sure to follow those disclaimer guidelines discussed earlier to let your readers know you were given the product to try out. You may also find some new followers for your blog at these conferences. Again, attend with business cards in hand, so you can help spread the link to your blog.

You can find blogging conferences in your state or niche area by conducting a quick search online. You can also find information about various conferences, especially writers' conferences, by visiting ShawGuides.com. By doing some Google searches for conferences, asking around to see what other bloggers are attending or recommending, and by looking to see if any blogging-related sessions are being offered at writers' conferences, you will likely find several that pique your interest.

BLOGGING NICHES

Taking one look at the variety of blogging conferences that are out there demonstrates the wide range of niches that exist in blogging. There are mom bloggers, tech bloggers, beauty bloggers, gossip bloggers, and many, many more. No matter what topic it is that you are interested in or are passionate about, there's bound to be a market for it. Here are some of the most popular blogging areas.

- Health and fitness blogs
- News blogs
- Technology blogs
- Food and cooking blogs
- Gossip blogs
- Fashion blogs

In choosing the niche you are going to enter, you want to make sure that:

- you are interested in it
- you are passionate about it
- you have enough to write about on the subject
- people are searching for information on the topic
- it is a revenue-generating opportunity

Many people worry about whether or not there is competition in the market already. But that's not something you should focus your attention on. If there's competition, that is fine; it means there are people who are looking for that kind of information. Don't shy away from your blog idea simply because there is competition out there. Take a look at the competitors and see what you can do differently or better, and then go for it.

LEARNING MORE

There's always something more to learn in the field of professional blogging. That's why it's important to network with other bloggers, follow other bloggers online, keep up on blogging news, and learn about new blogging tools. You may even find in the beginning that there are classes on blogging that interest you. Check them out, learn all you can, and at some point after you have experience under your belt, you can flip it and start teaching those courses as part of your salary-generating plans.

When it comes to being a successful professional blogger, you have to maintain a positive mindset. This is true of any profession in which you want to be successful. You have to know what you want, believe you can achieve it, and then work toward making it happen. You have to know that it is going to take effort and patience in order to become successful. Most people do not become successful bloggers, or experts in any field for that matter, overnight. If you have ever read Malcolm Gladwell's book, *Outliers*, you will be familiar with his "10,000 Hour Rule." This idea is based on research that suggests that becoming an expert at something isn't about talent. Rather it is about the amount of practice that someone puts into doing something to become an expert.

After 10,000 hours of practice, one should be an expert at what they are doing. The 10,000 hours may seem like a like long way off if you are just getting started. But it will go by quickly, and all along the way you will be learning more and gaining skills to further your expertise in blogging.

Becoming a successful blogger takes a commitment and patience, as well as the ability to overcome challenges. When entering any career field there are going to be areas that people have to navigate in order to become successful. They don't give up in a month or two and choose another career. They stick with it, find ways to keep going, learn all they can, see what works and doesn't work, and they continue on. That's the same way people should be entering the professional blogging field.

SECRETS OF SUCCESSFUL BLOGGERS

There are a lot of successful bloggers online, as you will surely find out as you begin to navigate your way around the Internet. You will also likely come across some of them at conferences, meet some networking, and hear some give talks on blogging-related topics.

Here some of the secrets of successful bloggers that you can keep in mind as you pave your own blogging trail.

- Know what you will cover. Get off to a good start by clearly defining your blogging niche. Decide what your area of focus will be and who your audience is.
- Have a clear idea of who your audience is. Who would be interested in what you are blogging about? You need to know that, so you know how and where to reach those people.
- Love what you are writing about, or love the money it is bringing in. Most advice you will get is that you need to be passionate about what you are writing about. But that doesn't always translate to paying the bills. You also don't have to do just one or the other. You can have a blog where you write about what you are passionate about, and you can do blogging work that pays the bills. Being passionate

about making a living as a professional blogger works every bit as well as being passionate about the topic you are writing on.

- Choose a good domain name. It needs to be something that is easy to remember, easy enough for people to spell, and preferably a .com domain name.
- Have patience. Successful blogs are not built overnight. It takes time to build up an audience and reputation, and have your blog showing up in all the search engines. In the meantime, while you grow your blog, seek out paid blogging gigs from other clients.
- Take measures to market and promote your blog, so you get your name out there. Whether it's using business cards, social media, or sharing the URL with every person you meet, you have to be active in getting the word out.
- Provide great content. People will come to your blog once because they stumbled upon it or were referred to it. But great content will keep them coming back. You need to provide them with something that is useful, interesting, funny, inspiring, or that they feel they just can't pass up on. Whatever approach you take, it needs to be good enough content to keep them coming back for more.
- Be consistent with publishing on your blog. Whether it is daily or weekly, you need to be consistent so that your readers know what to expect from you.
- Use SEO effectively in order to increase your traffic. While you don't want to have SEO choking your verbiage, you need to have some keywords here and there in order to help your audience find you.
- Try to keep your blogging of each post to a minimum time frame. If your blog posts each take a long time to write you

won't be efficient and may get discouraged. Try to keep it short (around 300 words or so), simple, and something that you can write with a minimal input of time.

- Maintain a positive outlook and attitude. If you believe you can do something, there is a better chance you will do it. But if you doubt yourself and your abilities, then you are setting yourself up to be unsuccessful. Focus on the positives and strive to maintain a good attitude about your blogging. Picture what it is that you want, focus on it, and work toward making it happen.

Many people wonder where and how bloggers can drum up so many blog post ideas. It's a good idea to have a pipeline of ideas so that you are always ready to go with the next one. There are many ways to come up with that pipeline of blogging topics. To help you with this, keep a running list on your desk and jot down ideas as they come to you, scan the news looking for new research studies or topics that are related to yours, talk to others about what they would like to read about, overhear conversations while dining out in restaurants, conduct surveys, find some statistics, conduct interviews, write book reviews, and make lists of helpful tips. The possibilities are endless.

One thing you don't want to do is throw your hands in the air and proclaim that you have "writer's block." While some people believe in writer's block, as something that prevents them from being able to write or determine what to write about, I am not one that believes in it. There is writing, and then there are excuses for not writing. There's no such thing as being "blocked" from being able to do our profession. Doctor's don't get blocked. Neither do lawyers, judges, taxi cab drivers, or any other professional out there.

If you find yourself feeling "blocked," realize that you just need to stop being distracted by the many other things going on around you, get your butt in the chair, and start typing. Or, maybe it's time for you to take a walk around the neighborhood, notepad in hand, and jot down a few ideas that nature brings to you as you are getting some fresh air.

LAST BYTE

"Failure is impossible."
—**Susan B. Anthony**

When I first threw my hat into the ring to be a professional writer back in 2004, some people were skeptical. They questioned whether or not I would be able to make a living as a professional writer and how I would pull it off. But I had no doubts in my mind that I would succeed at my mission. After all, I had been raised to believe that I could do anything I put my mind to.

Today I continue to make my living as a professional writer, with blogging making up a good portion of the work that I do. In fact, it increasingly becomes a larger part of what I do as more businesses begin to see the benefits of having a blog. I not only maintain my own blogs, and generate revenue from them, but I also do a lot of blogging for other businesses. I have clients for whom I write multiple blog posts on a weekly and monthly basis, the majority of which is ghostwriting.

When I dedicated myself to my writing career, I believed wholeheartedly that there was no way I could fail. I knew that I would succeed at making a living with my writing, and I just figured that I would navigate any challenges that came my way. It wasn't until about six years later when I was sharing this story with someone that she said I used the Laws of Attraction to get what I wanted. At the time I wasn't all that up on what the Laws of Attraction entailed. So I looked into it, reading such books as *The Secret*, which teaches that

165

if you set out to achieve what you want, the universe will conspire to make it happen. It's true! Even before I knew much about the Laws of Attraction, I had applied it to my life to get the career that I wanted, and still want today.

As you go forward and enter into the professional blogging field, my wish for you is that you maintain the same positive attitude. I believe that my positive outlook in approaching my career field has helped me succeed, as well as overcome the challenges I have met along the way.

Go into the professional blogging field knowing that you are entering a growing market—one that continues to gain in popularity, is going to be around for a long time to come, and one in which you can become an expert. All you need to do is keep on working toward reaching your goals, and practice—get your 10,000 hours under your belt.

Use your notebook of all the notes you took while reading this book, along with the tips and advice that are found throughout the pages of this book, to go forward and create! You *can* make a living as professional blogger. I wish you success in your journey!

Glossary of Blogging Terms

Adsense

Google's advertising network, from which you can earn money by placing the code for the ads on your blog.

Adwords

The advertising program offered by Google through which you can place an ad.

Affiliate Marketing

A revenue-generating option where you earn a commission on sales that advertisers receive from referrals from your site.

Aggregator

A tool that gathers data that has been published and puts it into one location. It usually helps readers keep up with their blog posts all in one place.

Alexa

A company that monitors the traffic information websites receive. You can log onto Alexa.com to get site traffic information.

Blog

A "web log," or a website that contains posts that have been published in a chronological order. The blog posts all have a time and date stamp, and may also allow for commenting.

Blogger
A writer who regularly composes blog posts and maintains at least one blog.

Blogging
The act of writing a blog post or maintaining a blog.

Blog Host
Also known as a service provider, this is a company that has the software capabilities to allow for publishing a blog.

Blogosphere
The blogging community, or all the blogs that are interconnected on the Internet; the culture that is made up of bloggers.

Blogroll
A list of other blogs with links to them, typically found on the home page of a blog.

Comments
Reader feedback that may be allowed following a blog post. Comments can be turned on and off, or can automatically turn off after a specified period of time.

Cost Per Click (Cpc)
A pay structure that many advertising networks offer, meaning that you get paid each time someone clicks on an ad that is running on your blog.

Cost Per Mille (Cpm)
The cost per 1,000 page impressions, the rate at which online advertising is usually sold. If you purchase ad space or sell it, based on the number of page views the advertiser will receive, it would be on a CPM basis.

Hypertext Markup Language (HTML)

The language that is used on the back end of a blog or website. Through the use of tags and code, it creates the page people see when they look at a site online.

Permalink

A permanent link that will remain even if the blog post has been changed.

Photo Blog

A blog that is made up of images and little text.

Ping

The action that is taken to inform a site that a blog has been updated and new content has been published.

Podcast

An audio file that can be downloaded and listened to on the computer or other devices.

Really Simple Syndication (RSS) Feed

Also known as a web feed, it is a way that content is syndicated on a blog.

Search Engine Optimization (SEO)

Using particular keywords to help your content be picked up more easily by search engines. Tags on the blog can be optimized, as well as the content in the posts.

Template

A site that has been designed for immediate use. All you have to do is add your unique content. It is ideal for those with limited technical skills or who do not know HTML.

Trackback

An option in your blogging software that will place a link to your post on someone else's blog if they have their blog set up to allow it.

Vlog

A video blog that focuses on having videos as the main attraction.

Web Ring

A network of blogs that provide links to keep people visiting one after another in a ring.

Getting Started: A Checklist for Success

- ❑ Determine why you want to blog and what your goals are as a blogger.
- ❑ Decide what to blog about.
- ❑ Choose your blog name.
- ❑ Find a good URL.
- ❑ Decide which blog host option to go with.
- ❑ Design your blog.
- ❑ Write your first post(s).
- ❑ Promote your blog.
- ❑ Monetize your blog.
- ❑ Set goals and measure success.
- ❑ Grow your business.
- ❑ Be a part of the blogging community.

Index

re-blogging, 89
return on investment (ROI), 146,
    151
RSS. *See* Really Simple
    Syndication

S
search engine optimization
    (SEO), 43, 63, 74, 91–96, 133,
    151, 163
SEO. *See* Search engine
    optimization
serial blogging, 22, 29, 30, 134
SethGodin.typepad.com, 25, 115
sharing options, 149–150
ShawGuides.com, 159
skills of blogger, 16–17
S.M.A.R.T. goals, 15
social media, 17, 88, 97, 103, 145,
    149. *See also* Facebook; Twitter;
    Pinterest
        blogs as, 63
social security number, 143
sponsorships, 147
subscriptions, blog, 88–91, 109
success, measure of, 109–111
successful bloggers, 22–25,
    162–165

T
taxes
        deductions, 142, 143–144
        filing, 140
        tax identification number,
        143
TechCrunch.com, 25, 115
Technorati, 149
templates, design, 47

TMZ.com, 25
topics, 164
traffic to blog, 86–87, 105–109
        email subscriptions, 88–91
        finding audience, 87–88
        using SEO for building,
        91–96
TreeHugger.com, 24, 115
Twitter, 88, 97, 149
Typepad, 45

U
uniform resource locator (URL),
    40–44
URL. *See* uniform resource
    locator

V
veganblogs.org, 1 49
Vistaprint, 150
vlogging, 71–74
VolusiaCountyMoms.com, 21, 40

W
Weblog, 4
website versus blog. *See* blog ver-
    sus website
widgets, 79–80, 99–100
WordPress, 45–46
Wordtracker, 33
writer's block, 164
writing blog posts
        About page, 54
        bolding, 65
        bullets, 64
        first post, 52–54
        headlines, 64
        short sentences, 65

style, 65
subheadings, 64
writing voice, 60

Y

Yahoo! Groups, 156

YouTube, 97, 149

Z

ZenHabits.net, 24, 67, 98, 115

Books from Allworth Press

Allworth Press is an imprint of Skyhorse Publishing, Inc. Selected titles are listed below.

Branding for Bloggers
by Zach Heller (5 ½ x 8 ½, 112 pages, paperback, $16.95)

Starting Your Career as a Freelance Writer, Second Edition
by Moira Anderson Allen (6 x 9, 304 pages, paperback, $24.95)

Starting Your Career as a Freelance Web Designer
by Neil Tortorella (6 x 9, 256 pages, paperback, $19.95)

Starting Your Career as a Freelance Editor: A Guide to Working with Authors, Books, Newsletters, Magazines, Websites, and More
by Mary Embree (6 x 9, 240 pages, paperback, $19.95)

Starting Your Career as a Social Media Manager
by Mark Story (6 x 9, 264, paperback, $19.95)

Publish Your Book: Proven Strategies and Resources for the Enterprising Author
by Patricia Fry (6 x 9, 264, paperback, $19.95)

The Pocket Small Business Owner's Guide to Starting Your Business on a Shoestring
by Carol Tice (5 ¼ x 8 ¼ , 224 pages, paperback, $14.95)

The Writer's Legal Guide
by Kay Murray and Tad Crawford (6x 9, 352 pages, paperback, $19.95)

The Pocket Legal Companion to Copyright: A User-Friendly Handbook for Protecting and Profiting from Copyrights
by Lee Wilson (5 x 7 ½, 320 pages, paperback, $16.95)

The Business of Writing: Professional Advice on Proposals, Publishers, Contracts, and More for the Aspiring Writer
Edited by Jennifer Lyons; foreword by Oscar Hijuelos (6 x 9, 304 pages, paperback, $19.95)

To see our complete catalog or to order online, please visit *www.allworth.com*.